Contents

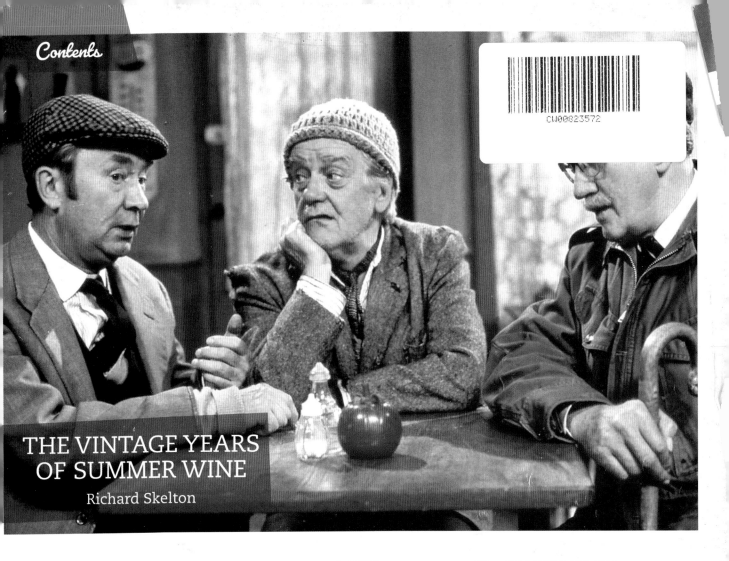

THE VINTAGE YEARS OF SUMMER WINE

Richard Skelton

Author:
Richard Skelton

Production editor:
Lucy Wood

Designer:
BookEmpress /
Craig Lamb - Kriele Ltd

Publisher:
Steve O'Hara

Publishing director:
Dan Savage

Commercial director:
Nigel Hole

Marketing manager:
Charlotte Park
cpark@mortons.co.uk

Advertising manager:
Sue Keily

Printed by:
William Gibbons and Sons

ISBN:
978-1-911639-29-9

Copyright:
©2021 Mortons Media Group Ltd.
All rights reserved.

MORTONS
MEDIA GROUP LTD

Acknowledgements

Holmfirth
(Jean Shires)

I have lived in the Holme Valley since 1991 and first stayed here as a visitor in 1978, furthermore, I worked in the television industry for many years. Consequently, I am particularly aware of the popularity of Last Of The Summer Wine and its close relationship with the town of Holmfirth. Nonetheless, I do not pretend for one moment to be a Summer Wine superfan or an encyclopaedic series expert. In any event, this bookazine is not intended to be a definitive history of the show. It is instead, I hope, an accessible and celebratory account of this amazing series, told partly from a Holme Valley point of view.

The bulk of the spectacular photographs in this publication have been supplied by Summer Wine photographer Malcolm Howarth, who has collaborated with me on this project. We are deeply indebted to Malcolm's friend, Don Smith, a fellow freelancer who has granted permission to use a good number of his pictures from the early years. Further archive images are from Bill Owen's personal collection. Additionally, photographs have been supplied by four talented Holme Valley photographers: Howard Allen, Dave Nussey, Andrew Sanderson, and Jean Shires.

I am also grateful to the show's writer, Roy Clarke, for permission to quote from some of his marvellous scripts, and to Holmfirth artist Jenny Hinchliffe for allowing me to use some of her wonderful sketches and drawings, as well as agreeing to be interviewed. Jenny's recollections are quoted in the text along with those of Malcolm Howarth and long-term Holmfirth residents Jack and Beryl Dunnill. Thanks to all.

Grateful acknowledgment is also due to Bob Fischer (summerwinos. co.uk) and local history enthusiast David Cockman for their help in tracking down historic images, and to Terry Bartlam of summerwine.net, who has supplied pictures, knowledge and advice.

Andrew Vine's authoritative book, Last Of The Summer Wine (2010, Arum Press) was invaluable in my research, and Jack Dunnill's Summer Wine Souvenir Guide provided useful written material.

My wife, Loretta, has been supportive over several months, first as a sounding board for ideas, then later as an eagle-eyed proofreader.

Finally, I would like to acknowledge publisher Steve O'Hara for his patience and professionalism, and the multi-talented team at Mortons that put this special bookazine together.

In Sid's Café
(Malcolm Howarth)

Last Of The Summer Wine is the longest-running comedy series in television history and has touched the hearts of many millions of people around the world. The first episode was broadcast in early January 1973. It was, in itself, a one-off programme, but it turned out to be the first of a series of 295 episodes produced over an incredible 38-year span. In the 1980s and 1990s the show regularly attracted 12 million viewers in the UK, and Christmas specials drew even bigger audiences. Sir Terry Wogan was a fan, and it was reportedly the Queen's favourite programme. It has also proved enduringly popular in many English-speaking countries around the world, with repeats being shown regularly to this day in Australia, New Zealand, Canada, and the USA.

Last Of The Summer Wine can be called whimsical, gentle, and old-fashioned, but it is also thoughtful, clever, and witty, not to mention hilariously funny. While grounded in the everyday, it can be wonderfully surreal. It can also be rather non-PC, and surprisingly risqué! Central to the programme for many years were its principal male characters. These changed from time to time, but the most famous line-up was Compo Simmonite, Norman Clegg and Foggy Dewhurst, played by Bill Owen, Peter Sallis and Brian Wilde respectively. Together with the indomitable Nora Batty (Kathy Staff), these four can safely be described as among the best-loved characters on British television. While Sallis remained

on the show throughout its existence, and Owen until his death in 1999, the mismatched male trio was completed by four very different but equally brilliant British actors during the first 30 years. At the beginning, before the inimitable Brian Wilde joined the series in 1976, the role of 'third man' was played with aplomb by Michael Bates as Blamire, and while Wilde took a five-year sabbatical from 1985, Shakespearean actor Michael Aldridge joined the cast as mad inventor Seymour Utterthwaite. After Wilde left once more in 1997, Frank Thornton reported for duty as 'Truly of the Yard', retired police inspector Herbert Truelove.

But whatever the leading line-up, the three main male characters were ageing adolescents – old men refusing to be old and proving by their actions that age is no barrier to having fun. They turned the beautiful Holme Valley in the Yorkshire Pennines into a fantastical playground for their madcap schemes and hare-brained adventures. In later years, the series had more of an ensemble cast, something of a Who's Who of classic British comedy which included stars such as Norman Wisdom, Russ Abbot, June Whitfield, and Thora Hird.

Last Of The Summer Wine always made much of the spectacular Pennine scenery of the Holme Valley and the historic charms of the market town of Holmfirth: Summer Wine Country, as it has become known. It can be bleak –grim up North and all that – but it is also gloriously beautiful, with brilliant sunshine, breathtaking vistas, magical

golden light, and dramatic, fast-changing skies. Holmfirth is a former mill town built primarily on the textile industry in 18th and 19th centuries. It is 'real' and uncompromising, yet simultaneously picturesque, friendly, and welcoming.

Photographer Malcolm Howarth's first involvement with the show was in its early years. Having been sent on assignments for the Holme Valley Express newspaper, he got on well with the cast and won the trust of the show's long-time producer, Alan Bell. This led to Malcolm becoming an honorary member of the crew, and from then on, he was invited to future shoots and studio recordings as the programme's 'official photographer'. Enjoying an extraordinary level of access over many years, and helped by the show's star Bill Owen, who became a close friend, Malcolm amassed a fantastic Last Of The Summer Wine archive. Some of his pictures have become famous and iconic images, and there are hundreds more in his collection. A great many are featured in this publication. Malcolm also appears in the text as an interviewee, giving a unique insider viewpoint on the lives and times of this perennially popular television show. Other featured interviewees are former Holmfirth business owners and long-term Holmfirth residents Jack and Beryl Dunnill, and acclaimed Holme Valley artist Jenny Hinchliffe. All three have stories to tell about the series and its effect on the big-hearted little town where it was filmed.

Richard Skelton

Chapter One

BEGINNINGS

Yorkshire screenwriter Roy Clarke, hailing from mining country near Doncaster, completed two years' National Service in the Royal Signals and afterwards served as a policeman as well as working as a teacher, salesman, and taxi driver – all before becoming a full-time writer known for radio and television thrillers and comedies. Commissioned by the BBC in 1971 to produce a one-off television show for a forthcoming Comedy Playhouse series featuring three old men, Clarke, by then aged 40, was not keen. But he had a liberating idea. What if the central characters did not let their chronological age define their behaviour? What if they behaved more like adolescents?

He set to work and came up with a subtly clever comedy drama set in the north of England featuring the following fictitious old school friends:

CYRIL BLAMIRE: Ex-army, retired water board official. Lives in digs. Stiff. Pompous. Looks down disdainfully upon Compo (for reasons, see below).

NORMAN CLEGG: Former Co-op linoleum salesman. Widower. Quiet nature with a dry sense of humour (something of Clarke himself in this). A middle-man.

WILLIAM SIMMONITE, KNOWN TO ALL AS COMPO: A small, rascally man who, as his name suggests, is in receipt of industrial compensation of some kind, or else dole money. Perennially scruffy and lazy, he has not worked for many years. At some point in the distant past his wife has left him.

(Howard Allen)

James Gilbert
(Don Smith)

Clarke called his new piece of work The Last Of The Summer Wine, a title which elicited immediate resistance from within the BBC, and the working title The Library Mob soon became attached to the project, referencing one of the programme's principal interior locations. Clarke's original title was reinstated before the programme's eventual transmission. BBC Head of Comedy Duncan Wood, who commissioned the show and gave Clarke his initial brief, liked the script a great deal. He handed it to experienced producer James Gilbert, whose career to date associated him with an illustrious list of top writers and star performers of British light entertainment, including David Frost and the Ronnies, Barker and Corbett.

The show was written to take place outdoors and on location with a definite sense of space around it, and this suited Gilbert down to the ground, especially as he had recently returned from shooting a film in the Australian outback which he found inspiring. But, like Clarke, he was not sure about having old men at the centre of the story, even despite the huge ratings success at the time of Dad's Army with its cast of doddery septuagenarians and octogenarians. Gilbert felt it would be rather depressing spending so much

time with people without much of a future, and reasoned that if he were to bring out the playfulness and childlike qualities in the central characters, it would be easier, and maybe better altogether, if they were a little younger. He visited Clarke at his home to discuss the matter. Clarke was amenable and adjustments were made to the script to make the characters more middle-aged.

The two men got on very well and other crucial matters were discussed, including the show's title (neither of them liked The Library Mob) and the filming location. The first of these

Jenny Hinchliffe
(Dave Nussey)

challenges was a battle that could be fought (and ultimately won) on another day, but the latter needed solving, and quickly. Gilbert and Clarke drove around together looking at potential towns in South Yorkshire and beyond in which to set the show, eventually settling on the Pennine town of Holmfirth following a firm recommendation from the comedian Barry Took. Took had played Burnlee Working Men's Club on the edge of the town as a young stand-up in the 1950s, and his act went down very badly. He had recently returned there for an episode of a BBC documentary series and found nothing had changed very much.

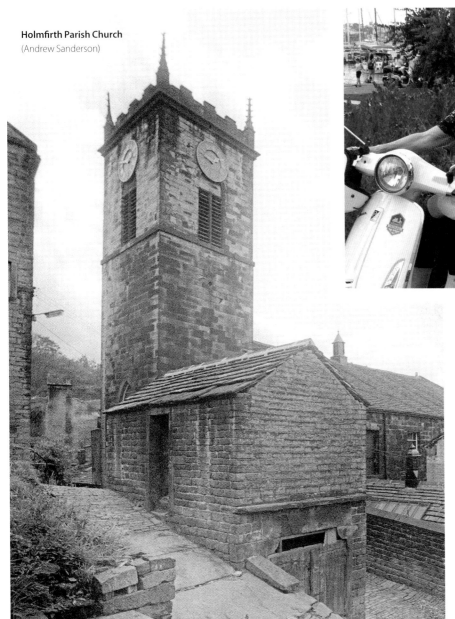

Holmfirth Parish Church
(Andrew Sanderson)

Beryl and Jack Dunnill

JENNY HINCHLIFFE: 'I came to Holmfirth as a young art teacher in the late 1960s, and the funny thing is I didn't like it at all at first. It was night when I got there, and the weather was bad, and as I came down into the town everything looked very dark and dirty and dingy. The mills were still standing and mostly still working, and I thought 'I don't know about this, have I made a big mistake?'

I'd moved from Bristol, you see, where everything was comparatively pristine. But when I had been here a week I fell in love with Holmfirth. I thought it was wonderful, and I came to love the people. It has always been a very unusual place, like some other little towns that are a bit cut off, but it is somewhere people have come and settled. It was always quite a busy little place. It's never been inward-looking, in my opinion.

HOLMFIRTH

Holmfirth was a tough little town founded on textiles and surrounded by spectacular hill country. Jack and Beryl Dunnill grew up in nearby Huddersfield and Netherton respectively, and Jenny Hinchliffe, appropriately as it would turn out, was originally from the Potteries. By the time of Gilbert and Clarke's visit, all three were living in Holmfirth; Jenny with her second husband Nigel, a Holme Valley native.

BERYL DUNNILL: 'We moved to Holmfirth in the mid-1960s and the textile industry was still functioning to a degree. There were still mills belching out smoke, including one at Crown Bottom right in the middle of the town, where the Co-op car park is now, and it felt gritty and sooty and quite a bit more industrial.'

JACK DUNNILL: 'Yes, but within fifteen years just about all the mills and factories had closed down.'

Hinchliffe Mill
(Jenny Hinchliffe)

Major changes to Holmfirth centre in 1921.
Both photographs show the parish church
(Author's collection)

'A lot of Irish people settled in Holmfirth after the dams and the railway were built. Films were made here, and the filming and postcard industry (Bamforths) brought people in. And it's where people have come to go striding on the moors, even back in Victorian times. There were pubs like the Rising Sun and another one up near Harden Moss, and people used to go walking to them. But it's like everything else isn't it – things change. Towns are built on different things and some don't change that much, but Holmfirth was built on the textile industry to start with. It is on boggy land and so the town was not established until quite late. There wasn't even a church in the centre of Holmfirth until about 1600. It was the same with Huddersfield. Both towns grew in prominence because of the industrial revolution. Actually, going back to about 1500 there was a candle factory in the Holme Valley, but it was made out of wood and burned down. Fancy building it out of wood when there's good building stone all around! Holmfirth itself wasn't mentioned in the Domesday Book but Wooldale was, and Hepworth is an old settlement, and other villages around are also old. So people lived in the area there and they used to do their weaving at home. That's why there are so many old cottages with mullioned windows. The whole family would be weaving away, doing their bit. When I arrived, there were huge Victorian mills everywhere: one in the middle of Holmfirth, two or three in Hinchliffe Mill and Holmbridge, and more in New Mill and out at Hepworth. But as the 1970s went on the mills and dye works started closing. The place was dying off. Then Last Of The Summer Wine saved Holmfirth and, in time, made it a desirable place to live... people selling up in London and the south and moving their lives up here.'

BERYL: 'But there are people who are forever saying Holmfirth's not what it was before Summer Wine – that people were friendlier then, that people looked after one another and the shops were so much better, and so on and so forth. Well, there was a time when we went to a baker on the main street to get a loaf of bread. We were catering for a funeral.'

JACK: 'It was Saturday. I asked for a loaf of bread and the woman started laughing. "Ooh Ethie," she said, "have you heard this? These people want some bread at two o'clock in the afternoon".'

BERYL: ' "Have you ordered it? You what! You haven't ordered it and you think you can come in here and buy some bread..." '

JACK: '...in a bread shop.'

BERYL: 'That is how we found a lot of people in Holmfirth. And you'd go into somewhere, and Nigel [Hinchliffe] was guilty of this, you'd go in and say, "can I have...", and before you could finish they'd walk away and start doing something. "Excuse me, I just wondered if..." "Yeah, I'll be with you." And you'd be left standing there while they unboxed

Holmfirth: A town behind the times
(Andrew Sanderson and author's collection)

Scar Fold in Holmfirth centre. The steps lead to Nora Batty's home
(Dr Neil Clifton, Creative Commons)

something or priced something up. They seemed to delight in messing people about. Perhaps it was because we were comers-in. It was a very odd place.'

JACK: 'We came to Holmfirth in 1966 and we're still comers-in!'

BERYL: 'There were some nice shops but they tended to be expensive. In the middle of the main street there was a Wallaces, a general grocer, a chain all over the place in the Huddersfield area, but again, very old fashioned. And there was a Co-op department store. It was a time warp. People used to say you could always buy liberty bodices in Holmfirth and other ridiculous things, but not so much the things you actually needed. When I was eleven, I passed my exams to go to Greenhead High School in Huddersfield and my mother was told, "She'll need a good satchel. You've got to

Market Day
(Jenny Hinchliffe)

Jenny

go to the saddlers in Holmfirth, they'll make you one that will last." Well, I'd never been to Holmfirth. We'd to get a bus from Netherton where we lived, to Huddersfield, then another one out to Holmfirth, which seemed to take forever. It seemed to be absolutely miles out. So I got this satchel, and it was very well made indeed. So well made, in fact, that not only did I use it for five years, much later my father got it down from the attic and my younger sister went through high school with it as well. It did ten years' service and could have done much more.'

JENNY: 'In the early 1970s you'd walk down Hollowgate and it was a mess. Everything was derelict and there were sheds full of rubbish, but there were various specialist shops which were surviving because people needed them. There weren't any supermarkets. You'd got three or four Co-ops in the town: the Co-op tailors, where you could get fitted for a suit, the Co-op butchers, the Co-op grocers, and a Co-op chemist.'

BERYL: 'I think Sid's Cafe was a shoe shop when we first came to Holmfirth. And the Co-op had a lot of different buildings in Holmfirth. They had a haberdashery, and definitely a shoe shop somewhere.'

JENNY: 'Co-ops were rife! And there was a very good outdoor market on a Thursday where they eventually built a modern Co-op supermarket. I was only very young when I first came, and I'd got very long hair, and this bloke who sold fish out of a caravan used to say, "Here she comes, the Sunsilk girl," after a television advert at the time. He said the same thing every week.'

JACK: 'But when Summer Wine first came, Holmfirth was a very old-fashioned town, and all the shops up Victoria Street were set in their ways. They were unable to change their ways, and in the end, one by one, like the mills, they all closed down.'

CASTING

With the script tweaked, the location settled, and a filming schedule being drawn up, James Gilbert set about casting his new show. In the early 1970s Michael Bates was a star name and a much-respected comedy and straight actor, and Gilbert began considering him for the part of Cyril Blamire as soon as he read Clarke's script. Born in India in 1920, Bates grew up in Derbyshire and studied history at Cambridge until his education was interrupted by the Second World War.

After serving with the Gurkhas, he pursued an acting career, going into rep, and performing in Shakespeare and in the West End. In the 1960s he appeared in major films including Oh

Michael Bates
(Don Smith)

What A Lovely War, Clockwork Orange, and Battle of Britain, and he played Field Marshal Montgomery in Patton. His comedy experience included multiple roles in the radio sitcom The Navy Lark, while his blackface appearances as Bearer Rangi Ram in It Ain't Half Hot Mum lay ahead. The first transmission of that other classic – and arguably now infamous – BBC series would be in late 1974. Bates was an excellent technical actor, known for his sharpness and impeccable timing. In private life he held

strong, no-nonsense right-wing views. He had a distinctive appearance and a precise, clipped speaking style.

The part of Norman Clegg was also soon cast. Peter Sallis was a journeyman character actor, highly respected in the industry for his professionalism and thoughtful analytical approach, and for his acting intelligence and ready wit.

Although familiar to the public, he was not a household name. While serving as an RAF radio instructor during the Second World War, Sallis acted in amateur productions and he later won a RADA scholarship. His first significant stage role was in School For Scandal in Bath in 1948, after which he worked in theatres around the country including in a West End play directed by Orson Welles. In 1966 Sallis starred with Honor Blackman, playing a sinister villain in Wait Until Dark. Feature film credits in the 1960s included Charlie Bubbles, Saturday Night and Sunday Morning, and a number of horror films. On television he played the title role in The Diary of Samuel Pepys (BBC, 1958) and undertook character parts in major series such as Danger Man, The Avengers, Doctor Who and Callan. In the future, Sallis would go on to do much voice-over work and become the voice of Wallace in Wallace and Gromit films and television specials.

But significantly for him, back in 1972, Sallis had recently appeared in two dark television thrillers written by Roy Clarke, and consequently Clarke had him in mind for the character of Clegg as he wrote the one-off script for The Last Of The Summer Wine – something he rarely did. As it would turn out, knowing Peter and understanding and respecting his talents greatly helped Clarke in his writing for many years to come. But when Sallis attended the BBC's rehearsal rooms for his audition, the actor did not know of Clarke's favourable view of him. He was so keen to land the part of Clegg that he turned up in a shabby old suit, cardigan, and flat cap, getting into character straight away. Nonplussed, James Gilbert thought the 51-year-old actor must have fallen on hard times.

Bates and Sallis were duly hired. The two had worked together in the past and got on well, and now they looked forward to doing so again, but who would be the third man? Gilbert was certain a faded film star called Bill Owen was ideal for the role. Clarke and Duncan Wood were not at all sure. Born in 1914, Bill Owen was the firebrand socialist son of a London tram driver, with a reputation for being argumentative and quick-tempered. As a boy he entertained as a singer and dancer in working men's clubs. Then he worked in a dye factory while treading the boards in am-dram. Owen later spent time as a holiday camp entertainer and got involved in political theatre before being selected for army officer training at the start of the Second World War. But, after being injured in a disastrous training accident and heavily traumatised by it, he was invalided out of the forces. Following psychiatric treatment, he returned to acting. West End stage successes in productions such as Desert Rats, and The Way to the Stars with Michael Redgrave and John Mills, led to a contract with Rank in the USA, an arrangement which rather fizzled out. After returning to Britain he picked up good film roles as a character actor and

Peter Sallis
(Don Smith)

enjoyed further success on the London stage. Later on, Owen appeared in four Carry On films and played Alfie on stage, and although rarely out of work as an actor, he also found time to become a successful playwright and popular songwriter, penning hits for Cliff Richard and Sasha Distel among others. Despite all this, as he reached his early fifties, he began to feel he had underachieved. He was probably being unduly hard on himself, but the feeling persisted, possibly exacerbated by regrets regarding a failed marriage.

But more recently Owen had been making something of a comeback. Though he was particularly known for playing cockneys, James Gilbert had seen him play northerners on stage and had just cast him as one himself in Whatever Happened To The Likely Lads. In addition, several years before, he'd seen Owen cope with Spike Milligan's outrageous comedic ad-libbing while playing the ex-Goon's somewhat Compo-like scruffy servant in Oblomov, an achievement for which he held him in very high regard. Owen was 58 when the script for The

Bill Owen
(Don Smith)

Last Of The Summer Wine dropped on the doormat of his Brighton home and, after returning to bed to read it he began turning the pages eagerly, liking what he saw.

He had been in shows good and bad, and knew when something was well-written and, moreover, when a part was right for him. After he spoke to Gilbert on the telephone to express his desire to play Compo, Wood and Clarke bowed to Gilbert's judgment and withdrew their objections. It was a decision they would never regret.

Holmfirth from Cliff
(Jenny Hinchliffe)

Chapter Two

SUMMER WINE COMES TO TOWN

As preparations continued at the BBC in London and a script read-through was convened, word of the new programme reached the people of Holmfirth.

BERYL DUNNILL: 'I vividly remember a woman who had the shop next door to ours, the Cosy Wool Shop. She sold nothing but knitting wool, and old ladies went in all the time buying it. The wool was cheap and she had a very good business, but she'd get bored if there wasn't anybody in the shop and she'd come into ours for a gossip, which could be a bit of a nuisance at times. Anyway, she came rushing in one day and she said, "Beryl, have you heard?" I hadn't. "Ooh," she said, "it's terrible. The BBC are filming a new programme about three nasty little old men hanging around doing nothing. They're filming it here and they'll be putting it on television. Now what kind of an image does that give people of Holmfirth?

People will think we're backward, living in the sticks somewhere out the back of beyond" – which, of course, we were really, even in 1972. "Right, that's it," she said, before bustling off. "We're finished now." That shows the locals' negative attitude before the series even came here.'

Holmfirth from Victoria Park
(Jenny Hinchliffe)

Dirty old town
(Andrew Sanderson)

and singers, and a lot of them were well-known names, although usually just a little bit past the absolute peak of their fame. Bands like The Hollies would come to Holmfirth, acts like that, household names that people had heard of, and the clubs would be packed out every weekend selling pint after pint after pint.'

A DIFFICULT START

The first day's filming on The Last Of The Summer Wine was not a success. Rain disrupted the schedule from the beginning and two key members of the cast had a blazing row that evening. It was an inauspicious start. The weather in the Holme Valley can be gloriously sunny or miserably cold and wet, but more often than not, it is best described as changeable, with fast-moving clouds affecting light conditions and sudden showers sending people diving for shelter. Difficult conditions for filming, because scenes are built up with multiple shots while the action is repeated as many times as necessary. Continuity is crucial in all respects.

There was nothing Gilbert could do about the weather except make the best of it, something the show's directors would have to do for the next 38 years. Late in the day the rain eased enough for him to grab some long-distance shots with his principal actors. These were mute (i.e. no sound), so better than nothing but that evening he moved quickly and decisively to deal with his actors' disagreements once and for all. When Gilbert called it a wrap, the cast and crew trundled over the hill to their accommodation in a moorland pub near the Colne Valley town of Marsden.

JACK DUNNILL: 'It wasn't a complete surprise. Holmfirth was on the map to some extent before Summer Wine because of the postcard industry which was long-established. Bamforths' saucy postcards were world-famous, but they turned out non-comic ones too – street scenes, country views and whatever. Our neighbour, Brian, was one of the artists at Bamforths and he lived in a Bamforths house. I remember a year before this, his wife Joan saying, "Brian says the BBC were there again this week. They're always coming round." I guess that was Barry Took making his film about Holmfirth, the one which took him back to Burnlee Working Men's Club where he was heckled and had to contend with Sunday dinnertime strippers. It was a den of iniquity!'

JENNY HINCHCLIFFE: 'Summer Wine coming to Holmfirth was a happy accident because of Burnlee Working Men's Club and Bamforths. Wheels within wheels... Barry Took recommending Holmfirth and James Gilbert and Roy Clarke both thinking the town would be great, and of course they were all absolutely right.'

JACK: 'Northern working men's clubs didn't change much over the years and in the early Seventies they were still going strong. The Wheel Tappers and Shunters television programme was actually very true to life. There'd be turns on every Saturday and Sunday, and there'd be a chairman sitting in a corner somewhere, making announcements and using a gavel or a bell to get everyone's attention. There would be comedians

A wet and gloomy day in Holmfirth
(Dr Neil Clifton, Creative Commons)

Nobody liked it. The location was bleak and inhospitable, and the main bar was operating as a bawdy strip joint. Squashed into a snug room away from the pulsing music and rowdy crowd, everyone began to eat and drink, and the frustrations of the day came to the surface.

Bates made some provocative political comments that were strongly right-wing and Owen bit back immediately, in an equally forthright manner, from his ardently socialist perspective. Sallis, who was largely apolitical, tried to cool things down. But the argument escalated, and it became impossible for anyone else at the table to speak, or even continue eating comfortably. Finally, Gilbert stood up and ordered Bates and Owen outside. Addressing both men simultaneously, he said, "Listen to me. This is a great script, and it could well become a series providing a good deal of great work for all of us. Don't ruin it!" He told them to agree to differ and shut up, making it plain that if they didn't pack it in right there and then, he would seriously consider pulling the plug on the whole schedule and recasting their parts.

From then on, the show's stars were billeted separately. Bates was booked in at a new motorway hotel, Owen found himself a B&B somewhere in the wilds, and Sallis made himself at home in Harold Wilson's old room at the George Hotel in Huddersfield. Gilbert's ultimatum had the desired effect. From that point on, Owen and Bates maintained a perfectly polite and cordial relationship; highly professional on set, and friendly towards each other at all other times, even on social occasions.

After the show was edited, the programme's scored music and waltzing theme tune were written by Ronnie Hazlehurst. A former big band trumpeter, Hazlehurst worked for Granada Television before becoming a staff arranger at the BBC. Among his growing list of credits were many sitcom themes including The Likely Lads, Some Mothers Do 'Ave 'Em, and Are You Being Served?, and incidental music for the The Generation Game. He did a great job. The signature music particularly was superb. Melodic and sweet, yet with a touch of sadness, it somehow stretched time and conjured a sense of space, setting the right pace and mood for the story to come.

ON AIR

The programme was transmitted at 8pm on Thursday, 4 January, 1973, and began with a character called Mrs Batty hanging out her washing and talking to two other women while looking on as Compo's television set (as they were called then!) was repossessed.

This is the dialogue:

COMPO:	Hey up love! I wish you'd stay inside, Mrs Batty – tha knows it only excites me.
MRS BATTY:	That's all he can talk. Filth.
COMPO:	But fluently. And your Harold's that wrapped up with his pigeons. Give us a word of encouragement, Eunice, else stop flaunting tha laundry where I can see it. Wash days are purgatory.
WOMAN:	No wonder his missus went off with that Pole.
YOUNGER WOMAN:	It's no fun being lonely.
MRS BATTY:	He's not lonely. There's a gang of them. Hang about that public library. They've nowt else to do.
YOUNGER WOMAN:	Poor old soul. What does he do when the library's closed – without his telly?
MRS BATTY:	Her next door says he exposes himself.

That exchange sets up what was to follow, not just in the remainder of the programme but, as it turned out, for many years to come. Mrs Batty was played by Cheshire-born actress Kathy Staff, who attended her audition in Manchester only at the last minute, and was allowed to read only out of

Kathy Staff as Nora Batty
(Bill Owen Collection)

politeness because as she walked through the door it was clear to Gilbert she was far too friendly, smiling and pleasant, and she was nowhere near big or formidable enough. Compo's relationship with his neighbour had to be absurd and incongruous. But when Staff went into character she blew Gilbert away. She had a big strong voice, gave great facial expressions and could clearly dominate a scene. With added padding to bulk her up, she'd be perfect. She got the part.

Kathy Staff was 43 years old when cast as Mrs Batty, a one-off job that ran for the rest of her life. By force of her acting ability she obliged Roy Clarke to keep Mrs Batty, to change her first name to Nora, and to expand and develop her part. Nora Batty would give Clarke countless comedic opportunities through into the next century, and she would become one of the most recognisable characters in the history of British comedy. A grounded, down-to-earth person, Staff had a working-class upbringing. After starting in am-dram, she turned professional at 21 but then took time off when she got married, switching to secretarial work for steadier hours and income. Returning to acting as an extra, she had bit parts in Coronation Street, and won a small role in A Kind Of Loving. Later she was almost cast as a major character in a new ITV soap called Emmerdale Farm – television history could have turned out very differently. And she lived just thirty minutes from Holmfirth. Nora's home, 28 Huddersfield Road, Holmfirth, became arguably the show's most recognisable location and, like its bossy resident, was also a lucky find. It became a much-loved setting with boundless potential for humour, with Nora situated above and Compo living underneath in what is known locally as an underdwelling, forever nipping out or scuttling back in. Serendipity played a part in its choosing, as a different location was originally selected but then rejected on the day because the prevailing light was considered unsuitable.

The Last Of The Summer Wine was a critical success and one of only two shows from that series of Comedy Playhouse to be developed. A run of six episodes was commissioned. It would be a sitcom set mainly out of doors, which was Clarke's aim from the start, and because of that, Holmfirth and its countryside would star as much as the characters and the writing, with Clarke exploiting the benefits and opportunities of using exterior landscapes and locations. But this outcome had by no means been a certainty. The thinking in comedy at that time was exteriors were only to be used when it was completely essential to set a scene outdoors. In the open air, the environment can't be fully

Nora Batty's house
(Jenny Hinchliffe)

controlled, particularly the weather; and in a studio, multiple cameras can be used to speed up the recording process. Consequently, location filming is always expensive.

Furthermore, setting the show in Holmfirth involved accommodation costs and extensive travelling for the cast and crew; and adverse weather was clearly going to cause problems. Wind and rain added time to the schedule, and time was money. Three weeks' filming would yield only a quarter of the final running time. Studio scenes, essentially all the interiors, would then have to be shot in London, in front of a studio audience that, in the case of the pilot, had taken some time to fully tune in to Clarke's offbeat sense of humour.

For the series, 'The' was dropped from the show's title and Kathy Staff was immediately brought on board as a regular, as were John Comer and Jane Freeman, who played cafe owners Sid and Ivy in the pilot. Comer had come to Gilbert's attention in a Play For Today called The Fishing Party, playing a

seafront stallholder. A northern stand-up comedian turned character actor, Comer had a number of feature film credits to his name including the Boulting Brothers satire I'm Alright Jack (1959). His Summer Wine character, Sid, had a love-hate relationship with his sniping wife, Ivy, and was quick with witty insults. Although he generally got on well with the leading trio, they could irritate him on occasion. A theatre and television actress in good form, Jane Freeman also become known to Gilbert through The Fishing Party, though her scenes as a seaside landlady had not brought her into contact with Comer. Her Summer Wine character, Ivy, was a buxom, bristling harridan. Formidable, fiery, and quick-tempered. It has been said that her character was based on the real Mrs Roy Clarke? Surely not! Ivy did not tolerate unruly behaviour in the cafe, nor any criticism of the food.

Contrary to popular belief, the cafe was a wallpaper store before being used as a filming location and not an unpleasant fish and chip shop.

John Comer, Jane Freeman and Bill Owen in Sid's Cafe.
(Don Smith)

BERYL: 'The fish and chip shop was in the building at the bottom of the church steps that later became a delicatessen. It was run by a nasty man who used to spit in the fat.'

JACK: 'If it flew out again the fat was hot enough. If it stayed in, it wasn't hot enough yet!'

BERYL: 'He wasn't exactly thin, but the woman who worked with him, who most people thought was his wife and was actually his sister-in-law, was absolutely massive.'

JACK: 'Occupational hazard I suppose.'

JENNY: 'She was a huge woman. I remember they had a job to pass each other behind the counter.'

BERYL: 'And they had a cat that was also massive. Probably the biggest cat I've ever seen.'

JACK: 'There were queues a mile long on a Saturday night. The pubs would shut at half-past ten in those days and everybody would pile down to the fish and chip shop.'

CHARACTERISATION

With the principal actors in place, Clarke imagined hearing their voices while writing the dialogue, and the words flowed easily. It took him a fortnight to do an episode but found he could do rewrites and extra scenes to order much more quickly. The main characters developed, as did their relationships with each other, and their back stories began to be filled in.

BLAMIRE: Like the actor who played him, Cyril Blamire was patriotic and right wing. A former corporal in the Royal Signals who had served in India, he was bristling and abrasive, clipped and irritable, with an upright, military bearing. Faultlessly neat and well-groomed, he was usually dressed spotlessly in a smart blazer, regimental tie, and trilby hat. He was also haughty,

The steep stone steps by the parish church in Holmfirth. Sid's Cafe is to the right of the artist's perspective, and not pictured.
(Jenny Hinchliffe)

condescending, and prone to snobbery, often disapproving and especially of Compo. He could also be pretentious, and seemed unaware that his smug, self-confident self-view tended towards the unrealistic, given the evidence as to how humbly his life had actually turned out. Despite all the above, it is testament to Clarke's fine writing and Bates' subtle acting skills that Blamire was nonetheless an unfailingly likeable and sympathetic character.

CLEGG: Timid, nervous and shy, Norman Clegg was also sharp, witty and dry. The philosopher of the three, Sallis's thoughtful character would regularly make astute observations in a humorous way, frequently delivering Clarke's very best lines. Somewhat dowdy in appearance, Clegg generally wrapped up warm under many layers of clothing. The son of a builder and decorator and an overprotective mother, Clegg married his wife, Edith, in the 1940s, and she had died in 1971. In early episodes he was prone to reminisces about his marriage, and regularly mentioned his wife's sharp tongue. After her death and being made redundant from his job as a lino salesman, Clegg aimed for a peaceful retirement but found himself continually thwarted in this ambition by his old school pals Compo and Blamire. Although happy reading alone at home and finding enjoyment in simple things, Clegg began hanging around with his friends. The ageing threesome regularly visited Sid's Café, the library, and various pubs together, as well as embarking on numerous madcap adventures in the countryside around Holmfirth. Although generally more cautious and skeptical than the other two, Clegg would often go along with their crazy schemes in order to please, against his better judgment. And while he was a reluctant and anxious driver, having a valid driving licence resulted in him sometimes being pressured into chauffeuring the others around.

COMPO: Of unmistakable appearance – short and unshaven in a woolly hat, collarless shirt, tatty jacket, and grimy, string-tied trousers and welly boots – Compo Simmonite, scruff-pot keeper of ferrets and long-time admirer of Nora Batty, was set to become one of the great television comedy characters of all time. Brilliantly conceived by Roy Clarke and expertly realised by Bill Owen with deceptive deftness and skill, Compo was forever child-like and spontaneous, a boy-like man given to kicking stones and walking on walls and along the edge of pavements; a wild man prone to risk-taking, but also a shiftless, hunched old man, slouching, shrugging, dragging his feet, hands in pockets, malodorous, slovenly and plain bone

Laughing between takes are Bill Owen and Kathy Staff.
(Bill Owen Collection)

idle. He was cheeky, urchin-like, impish, and facetious. He was cackling and mirthful. He was spontaneous. He was chaotic. He was naughty and uncouth. He was leering and lustful – especially when observing Nora. He was impossibly untidy. His mother was a rag-and-bone woman. He was illegitimate. His brief marriage ended when his wife ran off with a Pole. One way or another he lived off the state. He was incorrigible, and totally unconcerned what anyone thought about him. He truly lived in the moment (although not mindful of Zen). He had a good heart. And it cannot be said enough that he was infatuated with Nora Batty.

NORA BATTY: For her part Nora Batty was also set to become a comedy icon: a bad-tempered, bossy battle-axe, soon to be recognisable nationwide and later by millions around the world. Padded out, made up, and kitted out in curlers, kindly Kathy Staff became fierce, hatchet-faced and fearsome, a man hater, and dreadful in her disdain for all things male. A scrubbing, sweeping, dusting harridan; a bustling, berating, shooing, foghorn-voiced, slab-faced monstrosity. She was big and plain, and cross and loud. She was sour, scornful, and forever scowling. She was formidable. She was unassailable. But somehow Compo was besotted, comparing her to Margaret Lockwood. By this she was appalled, but also flattered and bewildered. In bafflement she feigned disgust and disapproval.

The cast got on well, and they settled into their characters. Bates gave Freeman unsolicited help and advice on comedy acting. She didn't mind. Comer and Freeman had good chemistry; she shouting and sniping, and him returning fire with well-aimed potshots.

The pilot episode was repeated on November 5, 1973, and the series continued a week later with the first of the six new programmes. Critics inside the BBC felt there was a lack of overall narrative, and that the stories meandered. But, of course, that was deliberate on Roy Clarke's part. Maybe they just didn't get it… yet.

The audiences certainly approved. By the end of its run, the series was pulling an audience of ten million, double what it started with and just two million less than national favourite Dad's Army. Not bad going.

The original Summer Wine trio of (left to right) Blamire, Compo, and Clegg.
(Don Smith)

Chapter Three

ONWARDS AND UPWARDS

When a second series was commissioned James Gilbert was desk-bound as the BBC's Head of Comedy, and he put his assistant, former actor Bernard Thompson, forward as his replacement as director/producer. Shooting was delayed by industrial action at the BBC, perhaps giving the new man time to consider a slightly different approach. Following discussions between Thompson and Clarke, the scripts for the second series had a different 'feel'. Dialogue scenes were generally shorter and there was more visual comedy. This more physical style required hiring stuntmen for escapades involving various means of transportation, but the three main characters were not replaced for scenes in the penultimate episode, in which they paddled a canoe down the fast-flowing River Wharfe.

The boat capsized, tipping all three men into the river, an event which was particularly frightening for Peter Sallis who couldn't swim. Somehow or other, they all made it, staggering and spluttering to dry land, Sallis having inadvertently made use of Bill Owen's head as a stepping-stone as he floundered in choppy waters. Shortly afterwards, filthy and saturated, lying on the bank recovering, he was approached by a curious member of the public, who leaned over him and asked, "Weren't you Samuel Pepys?"

The second series was broadcast in March and April 1975 and once again the audience grew from five to ten million during the run. This was perhaps a slight disappointment, but a third series was soon commissioned, with former Porridge man Sydney Lotterby drafted in to direct and produce. But before shooting could commence, Michael Bates reluctantly withdrew from the cast. After he was injured on stage during a medieval jousting match in a pantomime, a cancerous tumour was discovered. He was desperate to continue with Last Of The Summer Wine but after some months he still struggled to walk any distance. With the forthcoming series set to be more physical than ever, Bates graciously pulled out. After one more series of It Ain't Half Hot Mum, he stopped acting. Michael Bates died in January 1978, aged 57.

As the shooting dates loomed for series three, a new leader was required for the group – and a considerable degree of rewriting required to accommodate him. Roy Clarke came up with Foggy Dewhurst, another former soldier and

Brian Wilde as Foggy
(Don Smith)

commander of men. With encouragement from Peter Sallis, Syd Lotterby persuaded James Gilbert to cast Brian Wilde, an eccentric actor known and loved by British viewers as put-upon prison officer Mr Barrowclough in Porridge. Wilde was a Lancastrian, born not far over the border from Holmfirth, but he grew up in Hertfordshire, in London's home counties. He was bony and tall – six foot three inches – with a gangling, awkward way about him. Possessed of an expressive, gentle face with a curved chin, he was unusual looking, with a highly recognisable appearance and persona.

Although familiar to the public and professionally well regarded, Wilde was a respected supporting actor rather than a star name. Yet he was an exquisitely delicate and subtle comic performer; uniquely quirky and highly talented. In private life, he was a quiet, reserved cricket lover and real ale drinker. He could also be peevish, petulant, and pedantic, not to mention stubborn, as his new colleagues would eventually find out. Wilde was 49 years old when he joined the cast. Following training at RADA, he went into rep then radio

Seconds from disaster
(Don Smith)

Michael Bates as Cyril Blamire
(Don Smith)

work, making downtrodden characters a speciality. He appeared in the horror film Night Of The Demon and in top television series such as The Avengers, Dixon Of Dock Green and The Troubleshooters. Porridge, with Ronnie Barker, made him nationally known. His character, Prison Officer Henry Barrowclough, was kind, decent, gullible, and sad. Wilde played him superbly and the part made his name.

FOGGY

Foggy Dewhurst, first name Oliver, was, as Compo might have put it, a complete barmpot. Like Blamire he could be pompous and officious, and the two men shared a similarly inflated self-view. An ex-soldier, Foggy remained wedded to the minutiae of military life. He was a lover of rules and routines, a quoter of army manuals, and a stickler for regimental

discipline. He was also a fantasist. Nutty as a fruitcake. A hyper-animated, wild-eyed loon. He would often speak of his wartime military exploits in the jungle in Burma, frequently warning those around him that he was a trained killer and a master of unarmed combat. Stand well back, he'd warn them, or he couldn't be responsible for his actions. He was no such thing, of course. A former corporal signwriter, he was, if anything, an incompetent underachiever and highly unlikely to have ever seen combat.

Foggy was a deluded dreamer. A loopy philosopher. He was impulsive and emphatic; he could be petty, pedantic and mean; he was tight with his money; he could be nervous and cowardly. But unlike Blamire, Foggy was also irrepressible; a perpetual optimist who refused to acknowledge failure. He was a proud and earnest man, sensitive and easily hurt, meek and vulnerable with a child-like innocence which won the audience's affection. With great skill, Brian Wilde conveyed all of this, making Foggy Dewhurst absurdly funny, yes, but gentle and lovable too.

Wilde's first time on location was in early 1976, as the shooting of series three got underway. Entirely appropriate to his character, he wore an army-style field jacket with numerous front pockets, a regimental tie, and a smart cap. Well-polished shoes completed the ensemble, and he carried a walking cane. Blamire, it was explained, had gone off to Oswestry in hot pursuit of a recently widowed female of his acquaintance. A letter from him read out by Clegg reintroduced their mutual schoolfriend Foggy, who had

Compo, Foggy and Clegg. A classic line-up.
(Don Smith)

travelled in the opposite direction and arrived on screen soon afterwards being thrown off a Huddersfield Corporation double-decker bus.

CH CH CH CHANGES...

Foggy was not the only new character in the third series – Nora Batty gained a husband, Wally. That his name had been Harold in the pilot episode, and Nora's Eunice, was disregarded. Henpecked, naturally, Wally kept pigeons, his birds perhaps symbolic of a freedom he knew would never be his. Tending to them was an escape, and he was sometimes seen stealing an hour or two in the pub. Wally Batty was played by

Singing from the same hymn sheet.
Brian Wilde joins the gang.
(Don Smith)

Good friends in real life, Joe Gladwin and Kathy Staff worked well together as Wally and Nora.
(Don Smith)

Corporal Dewhurst, leader of men. While Foggy and Compo look completely at ease galloping across Holmbridge cricket green, Clegg seems less than comfortable.

(Don Smith)

Foggy falling foul of Compo's cousin, Big Malcolm, played by formidable Yorkshire character actor and former wrestler, Paul Luty.

(Don Smith)

veteran northern comic Joe Gladwin. Small of stature with a sorrowful, saggy face and a distinctive voice, Gladwin began his stage career as a tap dancer and comedian on Blackpool Pier. He established himself as a television actor in the 1960s and was well known as the voice of the Hovis television adverts. Wally did not altogether dislike the idea of Compo eloping with his truculent wife, and he could be sharp-tongued himself, although his occasional retorts would usually land him in even more trouble with Nora.

Joe Gladwin and Kathy Staff were already good friends and they worked well together from the start. Wally and Nora provided a second supporting couple to the main trio alongside with Sid and Ivy in the cafe, and Clarke was now writing more for them all to do.

The third series began transmission in October 1976 and was arguably the best yet. Viewing figures hovered around the ten million mark and Foggy, whose jumpy energy speeded up the show, became a firm audience favourite. Clarke wrote storylines that ran on across episodes and he introduced running jokes that Bill Owen would exploit for years to come, not least Compo's peculiarly erotic interest in Nora Batty's wrinkled stockings, and his delight in revealing the horrid contents of his matchbox to the womenfolk of Holmfirth. By now the cast and crew were a regular sight on Holmfirth's streets and embedded themselves into the everyday

BBC base at Crown Bottom, Holmfirth
(Andrew Sanderson)

What was in that matchbox?
(Malcolm Howarth)

SEEING IS BELIEVING!!
Call at
Nigel
Hinchliffe's
Holmfirth

Advert for Nigel Hinchliffe's shop.
(Jenny Hinchliffe)

life of the town. The Dunnills lived on the steep hillside behind the parish church, and Jenny Hinchliffe and her husband Nigel ran a newsagent and general store right in the centre.

BERYL DUNNILL: 'I remember we heard a commotion from our house so we went down and stood at the end of our front garden and looked over the high wall there onto the steep road below, called Back Lane. It turned out to be the Summer Wine crew. Because we weren't

in shot, we could stay up there and watch what was going on. They were filming Compo on a motorbike going down the lane over and over again. Michael Bates was there, and we chatted to him.'

JACK DUNNILL: 'A very polite man.'

BERYL: 'Bill Owen got on the bike at the top and set off, and then they cut. In a separate shot a stuntman came round the corner at the top of the lane and whizzed down the hill and out of shot,

where he supposedly crashed. Then they filmed Bill Owen again, lying there dazed.'

JENNY HINCHCLIFFE: 'My first interaction with Summer Wine people was when they came into the shop. It was handy for the cast and crew. I remember Syd Lotterby coming in frequently in the early days. Bill was also one of the first and we became very good friends with him, and Peter Sallis used to come in the shop too. I can remember getting Peter a cottage to stay in once. Even when I was

Laughing at Foggy's expense
(Don Smith)

building my own crockery business up, I carried on working in the shop once or twice a week and Bill would come in quite regularly and we'd have a good old chat. A lot of people would see us having a laugh together and took it totally the wrong way. They thought we were having an affair. What a load of absolute twaddle! People like to get a bit of scandal going and they make up relationships that don't really exist. We got on very well and he stayed at our house for a while, and his wife came up too, and Kathy, his daughter, for a bit of a break. They stayed at our house in Hade Edge.

'Actually, it was rather funny. I got a really odd phone call from Bill, the bicycle shop man in Holmfirth. 'Thank you very much Jennifer,' he said, 'starting rumours about you and me.' I said, 'What!' and he replied, 'My wife's really upset. People are saying we've run off together.' Apart from being completely absurd, it was a case of Chinese whispers. Somebody had said I'd run off with Bill Owen, and he was a Bill too. In

fact, I hadn't gone off with either of them!

'We were also on very good terms with Peter Sallis. I became particularly friendly with Peter, actually. We got on like a house on fire. He was lovely. Peter was more of a classical actor – in fact neither Bill nor Peter were considered comedy actors until Last Of The Summer Wine. Peter was witty and dry and very good company. They both were, and they both enjoyed a drink. The profession was like that. They were sociable human beings, and they were different times. But we didn't see much of the new third man, Brian Wilde. He was a loner. I think everybody got on with him well enough professionally, I believe, but he didn't hang about for a chat, or go out for meals in the evening.'

GOLDEN YEARS

Syd Lotterby directed two further series and two Christmas Specials, all of which were transmitted between November 1977 and December 1979, before standing aside to allow Alan J W Bell to take the helm. A former film editor, Bell had worked as an assistant director on the Morecambe and Wise shows, building a close relationship with the two comedy giants who so valued his judgment and opinions he was promoted to film director on their programmes. After directing film inserts for children's programme Crackerjack, Bell directed the BAFTA award-winning comedy series Ripping Yarns and the successful television adaptation of The Hitchhiker's Guide To The Galaxy.

The audiences for Summer Wine hovered around 12 million in the later Lotterby years until receiving a boost from two unexpected quarters. In 1979 Kathy Staff was also regularly appearing on British screens as cleaner Doris Luke in ITV's teatime soap, Crossroads. Popular broadcaster Terry Wogan joked

on his BBC Radio 2 breakfast show that Nora and Doris must be sisters. Much jocular chat followed in subsequent weeks, with listeners contributing via letters read out on air. Altogether this provided fantastic publicity for Last Of The Summer Wine and, reinforced by earlier episodes being repeated, drove a definite audience upswing.

An ITV technicians' strike was another gift to the show. From August to October 1979 the ITV network closed down and the fifth series of Summer Wine, which began transmission in September that year, moved to an earlier time of the day to take advantage. This meant cleaning up a few 'bloodys' in the dialogue but without detrimental effect, and with more family-friendly shows going out in an earlier, uncontested slot, audiences reached 20 million. By now Clarke knew and appreciated his actors' strengths to the full. He was writing better, more perfectly suited material than ever, with more two-part stories, razor-sharp dialogue, and even more visual humour, including side-splitting episodes involving a steam train and a hang glider. Clarke could clearly write brilliant visuals as well as dialogue – a surprisingly rare thing.

Meanwhile, Bill Owen had grown to love the character of Compo and the similarly scruffy town of Holmfirth, feeling completely at ease with both despite being an archetypal Londoner and, in real life, a smartly groomed, well-dressed man about town.

If anything, Compo was getting gradually scruffier as his costume evolved to its final and established form. His jacket and pullover gained extra tears, his tie was replaced by a kerchief, and a sash cord was deployed to hold his trousers up, replacing string. His stubble was kept uniform with a beard trimmer, and, from series four onwards, a collection of light green woolly hats

Peter Sallis was good company
(Don Smith)

Compo
(Jenny Hinchliffe)

A scruffy so-and-so
(Don Smith)

Becoming nationally known: Compo, Foggy and Clegg, and also Holmfirth
(Malcolm Howarth)

Bottoms Mill, Holmfirth
(Howard Allen)

from various sources replaced the darker original supplied by the BBC wardrobe department. Despite advancing years, Owen threw himself into physical, knock-about comedy with dexterity and aplomb. Happy to take risks in order to entertain, he climbed high ladders, walked on walls, and frequently fell down, off or into things. Exploiting his awkward frame as the congenitally incompetent Foggy Dewhurst, Brian Wilde also proved a most brilliant visual comic, and Peter Sallis's understated Cleggy was still getting many of Clarke's very cleverest lines and delivering them to perfection. By the end of the decade the show's main characters became absorbed into the public consciousness. Bill Owen was a star again. Brian Wilde had made another

great comedy character his own, and Peter Sallis was becoming a household name. Furthermore, the semi-wild Pennine countryside and the gritty town of Holmfirth began attracting attention from the show's fans, some keen to visit in pilgrimage, others even considering it as a potential holiday destination.

REJUVENATION AND RENEWAL

Partly due to Last Of The Summer Wine, Holmfirth was beginning to change. A gradual reinvention was taking place; one that did not immediately affect the nearby towns of Meltham and Honley.

BERYL: 'The town was picking up a little, but it was still a bit scruffy and down at heel, and as the mills closed down they

were left standing empty. It all started with the chimneys going. Before the mills closed many of them went over to electric power, and as the chimneys became neglected, one by one they became derelict and unsafe. So before the mills themselves were closed and demolished or repurposed, the chimneys started being pulled down. Fred Dibnah did at least one here.'

JACK: 'And as the old-fashioned shops closed, people weren't blaming the bad service and the poor stock and inefficient ordering, or even the fact that the mills were closing and people were travelling away to find work and do their shopping. They blamed Summer Wine.'

JENNY: 'Life in Holmfirth was driven by the mills. It was quite an industrial little town that was dying off and needed to reinvent itself.'

BERYL: 'But then good things started happening. Summer Wine brought the beginnings of a feel-good factor to the town. Better shops started opening, and we started getting restaurants.'

JACK: 'It's funny. People from Honley used to look down their noses at people from Holmfirth but that gradually stopped being the case.'

BERYL: 'They did. They were wild people in Holmfirth! When I was growing up in Netherton, we hated the Melthamers coming in. To us it was like the picts coming over the moors; and in Honley, I guess, they thought similarly about Holmfirthers.

JACK: 'They considered themselves sophisticates, and certainly within the Holme Valley Chamber of Trade, the shopkeepers and traders from Honley considered themselves the superior element.'

(Author's collection)

Honley
(Jenny Hinchliffe)

JENNY: 'Yes, the people in Honley certainly did think they were a little bit above people in Holmfirth. There was commerce and industry in Honley too, but Honley was nearer to Huddersfield and there was more of a village atmosphere there, and the town was less reliant on textiles for its prosperity.'

Holmfirth and the upper Holme Valley: ripe for renewal
(Andrew Sanderson)

Chapter Four

RINGING THE CHANGES

Starting with a special episode broadcast on Christmas Day 1981, and with the exception of one series, Alan Bell took control of Last Of The Summer Wine for 28 years and directed 250 episodes.

Coincidentally, just before being asked to take over the show by the BBC's new Head of Comedy, John Howard Davies, he had been filming in Holmfirth, shooting a segment for Terry Wogan about the town's connections with the early film industry. Bell had long been impressed by the spectacular scenery in the show, and after his visit to Bamforths Postcards regarding their involvement in pioneer movie-making, he was all the more keen to make even greater use of the countryside and picturesque aspects of the town than had his illustrious directorial predecessors.

JENNY HINCHCLIFFE: 'I remember Alan Bell coming into the shop before he started filming. He was in the area to get a feel for the place and an idea of how he was going to make things work. We were chatting at the counter and he said he was looking for locations around Holmfirth, places that were new and interesting, or where the scenery was at its absolute best, because he didn't know the area at all.

'Because I knew a lot of good scenic spots through doing paintings and drawings, I suggested a few ideas for places to go. I said to Nigel, "I'll look after the shop. Why don't you take Alan to see them?" That turned out to be a very useful exercise, I think, and he was forever grateful.'

Time spent on reconnaissance is seldom wasted. Bell displayed the vibrant, green Pennine landscape around Holmfirth to a greater degree than ever before. He featured the undulating farmland with its tumbledown drystone walls, the cool, dank woodland, and the windswept, heathery moors. He made use of the sparkling wind-lapped reservoirs, the deep-cut, babbling sikes, and the tumbling, fast-flowing rivers.

And in the town itself and the villages and hamlets nearby, he showcased the characterful cobbled streets, the charming country chapels, and the picturesque mullioned weavers' cottages.

Bell made series six more expansive than ever, creating space around the actors to exhibit the scenery. Benign weather conditions throughout the filming schedule aided him in his filmic endeavours – but not everything on set was sunny and set fair. Bell was a keen advocate of tracking shots, where the camera travels fluidly and silently alongside the characters as they walk and talk in a naturalistic manner, while the background changes behind them. There are two principal problems with this type of shooting: it takes a long time to set up the tracks for the camera platform, or dolly; and consistency and precision is required from the actors in terms of timing and placement. It was a directing style that caused difficulty for Brian Wilde.

In the past the final shape of a scene

Holme Valley view. Castle Hill, a Victorian folly, in the distance
(Jean Shires)

Nigel Hinchliffe's shop. Newsagent and general emporium
(Unknown)

would evolve, to a degree, during run-throughs and rehearsals, whereas now Bell had all movements and positioning precisely plotted out from the start. Bill Owen and Peter Sallis were more experienced on feature film sets and consequently far less fazed by this different approach.

Wilde adapted, although not without complaint, and Bell got the motion-picture feel he was looking for. The scenes came together well in the cutting room as he had planned, and the studio audiences liked what they saw during recording of the interior scenes at BBC Television Centre in London. Indeed, they seemed more enthusiastic and tuned-in than ever before, and a positive atmosphere was tangible throughout the process. The Christmas special, called Whoops, went out at 7pm on Christmas Day 1981, and was Bell's first episode. The script was nostalgic, silly and sweet, whimsical and warm and delightfully funny – a perfect recipe for Christmas Day family entertainment. Its audience of 17 million blew away all competition, including the feature film epic Gone With The Wind on ITV, the first time it was ever shown on British television. The 1982 Summer Wine series which followed was broadcast at 9.25pm on Monday nights until February 15, pulling in 15 million viewers and ending with what would be Owen's all-time favourite episode, From Wellies To Wetsuit.

Cinematic producer-director Alan Bell
(Malcolm Howarth)

Ready – Steady – Go!
(Bill Owen Collection)

Playing the same tune
(Malcolm Howarth)

a Batty day out!

(Bill Owen Collection)

Looking out over Holmfirth
(Bill Owen Collection)

Many great episodes followed over very many years, but in the future, it would be argued by some Summer Wine enthusiasts that the 1981 and 1982 series were definitive in terms of their overall excellence.

Last Of The Summer Wine was now firmly established as one of the BBC's all-time top comedy programmes and a seventh run was quickly given the green light. Bell, however, would not be at the helm. Brian Wilde had refused to work with him, causing an embarrassing problem for comedy boss John Howard Davies and the Corporation. To solve it Bell stood aside, and Sydney Lotterby agreed to make a temporary return. Bell took it on the chin. He was in strong demand in other quarters and, shrugging his shoulders, he went off to work with Spike Milligan, who had specifically requested his services. Bell would be back on Holmfirth's cobbles before very long, but until then series seven was in safe hands. The show returned to British screens on Christmas Day 1982 to yet more acclaim, with the rest of the series continuing to deliver reliable laughs in the first three months of 1983. Roy Clarke continued to work his magic. Not only were the show's main and supporting

characters wonderfully bonkers and brilliantly realised by the show's regular actors, Clarke also came up with hilariously off-the-wall guest and minor characters, often barmy and eccentric friends or acquaintances of the leading trio who would have crazy storylines built around them or make delightful cameo appearances. Drawing on his personal experiences as a policeman, teacher, salesman and squaddie, and on his rich working-class background, Clarke gave free rein to his fertile imagination and populated Summer Wine Land with a wonderfully dotty array of eccentrics.

Freelance photographer Malcolm Howarth had, by now, been sent on location several times by the Holme Valley Express newspaper and was a fan of the series. Later he would meet Roy Clarke on several occasions.

MALCOLM: 'He's got a terrific sense of humour, Roy Clarke, but he's such a dry character in real life you might not realise it if you meet him. He's not a jovial type at all; not a laugh-a-minute sort of fella. His sense of fun comes out in his writing. And if you read Roy's scripts there's nothing very complicated

about them. They're straightforward and simple, but hilarious. Simple, yes, but quick and very sharp. He wrote some killer lines. Wally Batty, for example – he came out with some beauties. Roy Clarke understands people, and what makes them tick. He's very observant, looking at life going on all the time, and even if you're with him you'll not realise he's taking it all in. The next minute, it's in one of his scripts.'

A GOOD FIT

Not everyone in Holmfirth thought Roy Clarke's fictitious personages were altogether and unfailingly funny. Some names have been changed.

JENNY: 'In the early years, a lot of locals said things like, "Ooh it's nothing like the people here in Holmfirth, I don't know why they've got to write such rubbish about us." Well, Roy Clarke didn't write about them at all, of course. He wasn't telling stories based on the people who actually lived there. He was writing imaginary things about imaginary people and setting the stories in Holmfirth. But some people there took it very much to heart. They thought he was having fun at their expense. The funny thing was some of the funniest and most eccentric people you could possibly imagine did live in Holmfirth at that time, and sometimes there'd be funnier things happening there than on the programme. There were more characters than in most places for sure, and enough of them for a sitcom on its own. There was a chap who'd have one too many at lunchtime in the Nook [a town centre pub], and in the afternoon he'd direct the traffic at the junction of Hollowgate and Victoria Street. He caused hold-ups and there were a few near misses but the police usually let it go. Dorothy [from the Wrinkled Stocking Tea Room] would take him off and give him a cup of coffee.

'There was Nifty Nel who married the millionaire owner of a minor stately home. She had a shop selling dainty dresses for little girls. Her own daughter was a huge lass. And there was Vera who would frequently leave her little shop unattended to talk to Beryl next door. Jean the Queen was the local traffic warden, a talented singer and dancer who'd be seen waltzing down the street in uniform with a little old man with a carrier bag over his arm. Jean was too kind-hearted to give many tickets. She let people off all the time. On one occasion I watched two drunks carrying a chest of drawers across the Nook yard, trying to avoid a puddle. Back and forth they went, and round and round, getting nowhere. Visual comedy at its very best.

'Mrs Boocock was a battle-axe, fiercer than Nora and Ivy put together. She used to scowl and say, "We're nothing like Last Of The Summer Wine!" In response

to a flasher she once said, "My dog's got one bigger than that!" She went with a GI in the war, so the story goes, and they found her knickers in a phone box. Betty Boocock, no relation to Mrs Boocock, would leave her shop to go to the Nook. She'd be away for two or three hours, the shop unlocked, and half her stock set out on the pavement.

'Eh What? was so-called because that was his reply to everything said to him. "Eh what?" The poor man had no legs, and he would trundle up and down to Holmfirth on an electric disability scooter. Had a sort-of skirt tied round with string. When his elderly parents died, he buried them in the garden. How on earth did he dig the hole? There was a right hoo-hah about that, as you can imagine. His wife was a bit odd too. She once let a guard dog out because she felt sorry for it and it bit her rather badly. There was a bicycle shop that held enormous stock going back a hundred years and had complete penny farthings in the cellar. There was the enormous lady and the gargantuan cat in the fish and chip shop with the man who spat in the fat. And once Jack and Beryl Dunnill were doing a house clearance and found a stuffed polar bear in the attic. There was no way to get it out. How did it ever get up there? There was a middle-aged couple that were, shall we say, rather on the large side. They were a bit waddly and slow-moving, but at a charity Come Dancing event at the Civic Hall there was a magical transformation. Smart in his penguin suit, with a number pinned on his back, he glided smoothly and

effortlessly around the floor, while she, galleon-like and stately in his arms up top, was all skippy and twinkle-toed below. It was fascinating and a marvel to behold.

'At the switching on of the Christmas lights each year, the town's Chamber of Trade would organise a torchlight procession. There was a chap in Holmfirth who looked just like Popeye, complete with his pipe. Popeye would always turn up, walking alongside the floats and shaking a bucket for his own good causes. He had nothing to do with the organisers. There were various disasters at these processions. One of the floats once took a power line down and there was a two-hour hold up. And on another occasion, someone jumped over a three-foot wall intent on relieving himself in a field. Unfortunately, there was a 20-foot drop on the other side, and he broke both his legs. Another long hold-up! So, you can see the programme was really quite a good fit for what was an eccentric and characterful little town.'

IN THE MOVIES

Alan Bell returned to the programme in style, arriving in Holmfirth in May 1983 to direct a feature-length Christmas special entitled Getting Sam Home. The script was, in fact, an adaptation by Clarke of a novel he had written in 1974. Bill Owen had been agitating for the book to be developed into a film for some time, and, won over by his solicitations, Bell used his clout in the BBC's corridors of power to smooth the way with the top brass. Not only was a long format, in-

The twinkling lights of Christmas-time Holmfirth
(Jean Shires)

Lynda Baron was Lily Bless Her
(Malcolm Howarth)

house, all-film sitcom spin-off something the Beeb had not attempted until now, the story was unlike anything the show had ever tackled before. An intelligent, dark adult farce on the subjects of death and sex, love and friendship, it was subtle, deep and full of pathos. Foggy, Compo and Clegg take their mate Sam for a secret night-time get-together with his mistress, Lily. He dies in action, as it were, leaving the lads with a problem and giving the show its title.

Having been surprised and impressed by Bell's on-screen results the previous year, Brian Wilde made an effort to patch things up with the returning director, and he joined Owen and Sallis to head the cast. Lily, or Lily Bless Her, as she was known, was played by Lynda Baron, an actress familiar to British television audiences and best known as Nurse Gladys Emmanuel in another Roy Clarke comedy series Open All Hours, which had been first shown by the BBC in 1976. In years to come Baron became a recognisable face to a new generation of viewers as the presenter of the highly successful 1990s children's series Come Outside.

Supporting couples Nora and Wally Batty and cafe owners Sid and Ivy also featured, but John Comer was ill with cancer and his voice was ultimately dubbed by Yorkshire actor Tony Melody. It was Comer's last appearance in the show. Jane Freeman continued as Ivy until the programme's final series in 2010, appearing in 274 episodes.

An invitation Sid would prefer to refuse?
(Don Smith)

On her very first filming day in 1972, Jane Freeman very nearly didn't make it to the location. In fact, she had only the vaguest idea where the location even was. Freeman told the story of her first ever journey to Holmfirth many years later in a piece she wrote for Jack Dunnill, editor of the Holme Valley Chamber of Trade Souvenir Guide. The article was entitled Highway To Heaven and she chose to recount events in the third person.

The sound of the alarm roused her from a deep sleep. She was still tired. It had been a heavy day yesterday, Saturdays always were. Rehearsals in the morning – they hadn't gone well, the matinee, and then the evening show. Now she must get up. What time was it? Oh no! Five o'clock. The car would be there in half an hour. She reluctantly got out of bed, washed, and dressed, and as she combed her hair the doorbell rang. "Won't be a minute," she called. With a quick pat of her head she reached for her coat and hurried down the stairs from the flat to the waiting car. Quickly she settled comfortably into the back seat. "I hope he's not a talker," she thought. "I can doze off on the journey." "Right love," he said. "Where to?" What did he mean, "Where to?" Surely they had told him where to take her. "I don't know," she said miserably. "I thought you knew." "No," he replied. "They just told me to pick the party up at five-thirty and that's what I've done."

She panicked. What could she do? How could she check her destination at five-thirty on a Sunday morning in the middle of Birmingham? There would be no one in the London office at that time. Hastily, she reached into her bag for the script. Oh heavens! Why was she so untidy? Oh yes, there it was. Eagerly, she scanned the typed script for some clues. Nothing. Ah, but wait a minute! When she had read through the script in London, she had played the character with a Yorkshire accent. In fact, most of the cast had. "I think it might be Yorkshire," she finally volunteered. "Right love, Yorkshire it is," said the driver. As they headed for the M1 she considered what to do next. After all, you can't just go to Yorkshire, can you? You have to be a bit more specific than that.

By now all thoughts of sleep were long gone. She was really worried. Her one day's filming on a new series and she was going to create chaos by not turning up! Once again, she reached for the script. wait another minute. What was this? A stage direction in brackets clearly stated: "Compo, Clegg and Blamire catch the Huddersfield bus." It was worth a try. "Huddersfield!" she said to the driver, "I think we should go to Huddersfield." "Right you are," he answered, willing as ever. By 7am they had reached the empty Sunday morning streets of Huddersfield. Now what, she thought, praying at every corner that green BBC vans would appear. Nothing. Just the odd early morning

A warm welcome from Ivy
(Malcolm Howarth)

churchgoer and tired shift workers hurrying home for breakfast.

Why, oh, why hadn't she checked the arrangements? Too late for regrets now! While she searched her mind for some new initiative, her thoughts were interrupted by the voice of the driver. "There's an all-night taxi office over there. They might know. Film people are always using taxis." It was an idea. Quickly they hurried into the smoke-filled office. Did anyone know if the BBC were filming in the vicinity? No. Somebody knew where Granada had been filming last week, but nothing was

known about the BBC. Just as they were about to leave a bearded man came through the door. "Hey George," one of the taxi drivers called, "do you know if there is any filming going on hereabouts?" "Well," said George, "there's the BBC over at Holmfirth." Twenty minutes later, as the sun finally broke through the morning clouds, they drove into Holmfirth. It looked to her like heaven! "Hello Jane," said the director. "Had a good journey?" "Oh yes," she replied casually, "it's good to be here." Yes, it was good to be in Holmfirth... a thought she has had many times in subsequent years.

CLASSIC COMEDY OF A DIFFERENT KIND

The movie-length special, Getting Sam Home, was classic comedy of a different kind and the leading actors all rose to the occasion, especially Bill Owen, who had a spring in his step throughout the show's four-week shooting schedule, delighted to be starring in a film once again. The show was transmitted on December 27, 1983, and was a critical and ratings success, drawing 14.2 million viewers despite being up against the tough opposition of Dallas and Coronation Street. As a result, there were extended episodes of other television sitcoms in the future. Last Of The Summer Wine had blazed a trail.

JOINING THE CREW

The Summer Wine crew grafted extra hard for Alan Bell to make sure Getting Sam Home was a big success, and the technicians on set now included stills photographer Malcolm Howarth, who had been invited to join the group.

MALCOLM: 'The White Horse pub in Jackson Bridge was a happening place and a hotbed for stories, and the landlord Ron Backhouse was an ex-miner from Royston near Barnsley, where I come from. I got on very well with Ron, his son Paul, and the whole Backhouse family. Ron was ahead of his time. The White Horse was one of the first food pubs, and the first pub in the area to do bed and breakfast. He turned it into a place to stay with about eight bedrooms. The Summer Wine people stayed there, and I got friendly with Alan Bell and the crew. I'd been on location a few times for the Holme Valley Express, but then meeting the people again back at the pub in the evening we became pals, and it became automatic that I'd turn up on set if there was anything exciting going on. I was given permission to use my pictures in the paper. Eventually Alan Bell said, "Will you do our official publicity photographs for us?"

Up to no good as usual
(Malcolm Howarth)

First day on the job. Three photographs from Malcolm Howarth's first session as Summer Wine's official Unit Photographer.
(Malcolm Howarth)

'The BBC would send top London-based freelancer Don Smith up maybe twice during a 13-week filming period. Obviously, it wasn't cost-effective for him to be there for any more than that. Besides, he was needed for other things. I liked Don and we got on very well. Of course, I said yes to Alan's offer and from then on, I was asked along every year. Getting Sam Home was when I began going onto the set in an official capacity. Before that I tended to set the pictures up off set. Now I had permission to step in and direct the actors in situ. I wouldn't have dreamed of doing that before I was hired by the programme.

'It was a bit daunting at the beginning. I remember my first day very well. There's a very steep street beside Holmfirth Civic Hall and I took some pictures there that have become classic images. Lynda Baron was there with her arms around Compo and Nora was looking on, less than impressed. Lynda Baron was super,

a fun person. I also did some of Nora with her arms folded, and then she did the matchbox thing with Bill. The day went well, and not only that, those pictures would come to be very important to me. There was no market at the time, but in the future those photographs would be a key part of my Summer Wine collection. They are still popular today.'

NATIONALLY KNOWN

Thanks to the success of Summer Wine and the nation's affection for his inspired portrayal of Roy Clarke's impish creation Compo Simmonite, Bill Owen was a star once again – perhaps more so than ever before. He appeared on This Is Your Life and was in demand for television, magazine, and newspaper interviews. All this proved good publicity for the series and Holmfirth, as well as for Owen's extensive charity work, for which he received an MBE. Peter Sallis and Brian Wilde were being stopped in the street,

and Nora Batty, too, was a national figure, with a Fleet Street newspaper giving away bumper stickers of the Holmfirth harridan. But it was Compo whom the nation truly took to their hearts, and Owen who was most loved and adored.

Owen continued to live in London and Brighton, but he really loved Holmfirth. He identified with the town and felt, somehow, he'd been there before, that he knew the place, and that it was his spiritual home. It was an unpretentious, working-class town – at least that's how it seemed to him. He loved the beautiful rural landscape around it and that there was still some industry, and the township's proud industrial heritage. The town loved him too, or, at least, the majority of its residents did. Owen felt he belonged in Holmfirth. He certainly wanted to belong, and on his days off during filming he carried out charitable work for local good causes of all kinds. And when he was away he never wasted an opportunity to promote Holmfirth, acting as an ambassador for the Yorkshire town he had grown to love more with each passing year, but that had felt special to him from the first time he set foot in it on a rainy summer's day in 1972.

NATIONAL CONSCIOUSNESS

Summer Wine was becoming part of the national consciousness and its stars were increasingly in demand for personal appearances. In 1982 Britain's kids voted it the funniest show on television and Bill Owen received the award on Noel Edmonds' Multi-Coloured-Swap-Shop. Owen and Kathy Staff performed in pantomime, separately and together. They also turned up on the crazy television game show It's A Knockout

Loveable rogue Compo Simmonite
(Don Smith)

F rom a perspective of 16 years, Bill Owen wrote about his first day in Holmfirth as his contribution to Jack Dunnill's 1988 Holme Valley Chamber of Trade Souvenir Guide. His piece was entitled My Dream Holme and he introduced it as "a few words about a subject I am never tired of discussing - my relationship with Holmfirth".

It was 16 years ago when I first came to Holmfirth to film for the pilot episode of Last Of The Summer Wine with Peter Sallis and Michael Bates. James Gilbert, who was also responsible for the original idea for the series, was the director. Up to that moment my only knowledge of Yorkshire was as an actor touring with a play in those cities and towns which boasted a theatre. I'd never heard of Holmfirth. Yet there I was on this spring day, having just arrived and sitting round the fire with the others in the Elephant and Castle pub.

And as I sat, I had a feeling that I'd been there before. I couldn't explain it and it certainly had never happened to me previously in my life. There was no logical reason for it... but in all the years it has never left me. I've always felt very much part of Holmfirth, far more than London where I was born and still live. Because of this inexplicable affinity, I even found myself speaking with a Yorkshire accent. It was unintentional. It just seemed to come naturally. And that's how it's been ever since, as soon as I arrive in Holmfirth.

It also seemed perfectly natural that I should become involved with the town and its people. I enjoyed being there and I wanted to belong. And I know the people have accepted me. I feel at home in Holmfirth. There have been many improvements in the town over the past 16 years, due in no small measure to its association with Summer Wine. But equally no one can deny that Holmfirth and the glories of the surrounding countryside have been contributory factors to the success of the BBC's longest-running comedy series.

I would advise any stranger to our town to visit the landmarks made famous by Last Of The Summer Wine and then explore the rest of the valley... the unspoiled hamlets, green fields, quaint streets, and meandering streams. Absorb the atmosphere... and then you will see why I love it. When we are filming in the summer, Saturday is our day off. But not for me. There is always some event at which I have promised to make an appearance, to declare something officially open, or to judge or speak. Indeed, since I was made President of Holmfirth ATC Squadron there are meetings to attend for our summer fayre.

But I always reserve some part of the day to renew my acquaintance with my town. Just the simple things like collecting laundry, then meeting a few of my many friends over a coffee or a pint and a pub lunch. These are the couple of hours of the week I wouldn't miss for anything. So, you see, my relationship with Holmfirth is very strong and I trust will continue long after the last episode of Last Of The Summer Wine.

and appeared as guests on Terry Wogan's peak-time BBC1 chat show, Wilde having refused two invitations.

The show's three male stars performed together in a sketch at the 1984 Royal Variety Performance, and Owen and Staff joined forces to record a single called Nora Batty's Stockings, which soon slipped down the charts. Peter Sallis and Owen both returned to the West End to good reviews, and a Summer Wine strip cartoon ran in the Daily Star newspaper. Members of the public wrote to the cast, some seeming to think the characters were real and their escapades matters of fact. There were also letters to the BBC praising the producers for the uplifting effect of the show; thanking them for taking older people seriously, and as having something still to offer, for portraying the show's ageing stars as still vigorous and full of life, for encouraging a new attitude to old age - one that inspired older people to get up from their armchairs and get out to do things.

TROUBLE AT T'MILL

The next series of Last Of The Summer Wine was filmed during 1984 and broadcast the following February and March, following a Christmas Special on December 30. On location, forced together for prolonged periods away from family and home comforts, stuck in a truck in the rain, tensions were rising among the show's main stars. By now a Winnebago was supplied for the three men, with a compartment for each. The supporting cast had to make do sharing a bus, with another large vehicle providing

a base and shelter for the crew, extras, and the show's wider entourage. Between scenes Peter Sallis busied himself with the Times crossword. Owen spent his time line-counting the script, displeased if anyone had more to say than him. And when not going through his own lines, Wilde drifted off, daydreaming. Owen and Wilde irritated each other and were not getting on. Sallis, for the most part, humoured the pair of them, a middle-man in real life as well as on screen. But he could be tetchy too, on occasion. Owen acted like a star, as if it were his show, but he was unfailingly good to work with,

taking direction without demur. Off set, he kept himself to himself most of the time, but he could occasionally be a little spiky, curmudgeonly, and defensive.

Wilde got annoyed because Owen had a habit of approximating lines, and in the studio he would even mess up on purpose to win the audience over, getting them onside to cultivate bigger laughs later on. Off duty, Owen was also prone to sermonising, giving vent to his strongly-held political opinions. For his part, Wilde began objecting to parts of the script, frequently pointing out things he disagreed with to Bell. Wilde

Suits you sir!
(Don Smith)

Bill and Peter were still happy in Holmfirth, while Brian considered stepping down
(Malcolm Howarth)

Summer Wine's most famous leading trio, but all good things come to an end
(Don Smith)

could also be a pain in other respects. He acted as his own agent and bargained hard over money, expecting greater remuneration than the other two. Word got out about this, souring relationships further. Wilde had said he was leaving after series seven, demanding rewrites as a condition of staying on. But he eventually signed after former Porridge actor Fulton Mackay was sounded out as a replacement character, a move which scared Wilde into line over the scripts (Bell and Clarke had refused to budge), and weakened his hand regarding contract negotiations. So Wilde could be stubborn regarding money and awkward over artistic considerations, and Sallis, too, had fixed ideas about how his scenes should be played, and didn't like being contradicted. But in fairness, Bell would concede, when Sallis made a stand about something he was usually right.

Syd Lotterby had given the show's tetchy stars a bit of a dressing down two years before, echoing James Gilbert's stern words back in 1972. But bad feeling remained close to the surface when the

three leading men reconvened in the Holme Valley for the shooting of series eight. The trio certainly did not socialise or eat together after work. Wilde stayed at the Hilton by the M62 motorway, Sallis stayed in the Huddersfield Hotel in the centre of that town, and for many years Owen rented the same modest bungalow in Underbank on the outskirts of Holmfirth, establishing a homely evening routine of a relaxing bath, a warming whisky, and an oven-cooked ready meal, such as they existed at the time.

The men rubbed along for a while. Then an unscrupulous journalist betrayed Wilde by printing comments about the men's dirty laundry that the actor had made clear were off the record. As a result, the trio's peccadilloes were suddenly very much in the public domain, and Wilde's relationship with Owen worsened. Although seething, Owen played it down, keeping up appearances, to coin a phrase, as the Press descended on him, desperate to get his side of the story. Brushing probing questions aside, he explained he and

Wilde were simply unalike. They differed, that was all, and while it was true that they had nothing much in common outside work, he maintained everyone always made an effort to get along.

Wilde was proved wrong to have wanted rewrites. Clarke's scripts were as excellent as ever and the characters' dialogue was consistently sharp. The first episode of series eight pulled an astonishing 18.8 million viewers and, overall, Last Of The Summer Wine was the second-most watched BBC programme of the year, beaten only by Clarke's own Open All Hours. But the last episode of the series, entitled Who's Looking After The Cafe Then?, broadcast on March 17, 1985, would to be Foggy's last appearance for some time. Wilde made it clear, this time he really was leaving for pastures new, and a new central character would have to be found.

Wilde would be a tough act to follow. Corporal Foggy Dewhurst was as finely-drawn and much-loved a sitcom character as ever existed, and Wilde was a quite masterful comic actor, subtle and understated in his performance to the extent even a complete lack of expression would convey a wealth of complex meaning. In the show, Foggy left to run a family egg painting business in Bridlington. He would later return before leaving again, this time permanently, to live in Blackpool, after an inadvertent proposal of marriage.

As Compo's popularity held steady, that of Nora Batty grew to match it, with Nora becoming so famous that Staff became very much in demand for opening fetes, starting marathons and myriad other guest appearances. That Staff was generally not recognised as she went about her everyday life was testament to her acting abilities and the skills of the BBC hair, make-up and costume departments. To play Nora she was padded out like a pantomime dame, to appear larger and bustier than in person, as well as being decked in a pinny, curlers, and those iconic wrinkled

Kathy Staff was an easy-going woman, Nora Batty less so
(Malcolm Howarth)

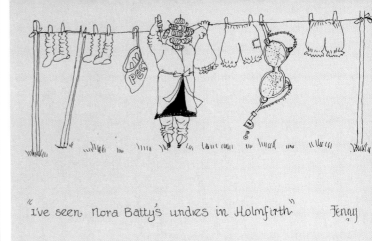

Early 1980s cartoon postcards by Jenny Hinchliffe, now highly collectable
(Jenny Hinchliffe)

stockings, and wearing a permanent scowl.

Staff was a friendly, easy-going woman. A true and devout Christian, she was unfailingly kind, considerate and gentle, in many ways the complete antithesis of Nora. But she was no pushover and would call a spade a spade. Despite her uncomplaining nature, she and Jane Freeman were just slightly peeved that the show's three leading men got two dressers, while the rest of the cast had to make do with one between them. Staff's increasing fame was later acknowledged, and she eventually got her own location caravan.

By now Nora and Ivy were getting more scenes together, working well as a fearsome female double act. They got on great off the set too. During studio weeks, Staff and Freeman would go shopping together in London after rehearsals; and when filming in Yorkshire the two would eat lunch in Staff's car, finding a moment or two of peace and quiet, and Freeman began staying overnight at Staff's home, just half an hour away, over the tops in Cheshire.

FIRM FRIENDS AND SOUR GRAPES

Jenny and Nigel Hinchliffe and Jack and Beryl Dunnill were among a number of Holmfirth residents who developed firm friendships with members of the Summer Wine cast and crew. But while some locals were keen to exploit a golden opportunity provided by the show for promoting the town and attracting visitors, not all Holmfirth's citizens and business owners were so inclined. The council too, was slow to take advantage.

BERYL: 'We were members of the Holmfirth Chamber of Trade and all the members wanted more people to come to the town. We were always discussing ways of advertising and promoting Holmfirth, but Kirklees Council was not interested in helping us at all. The council would not do anything to promote tourism or help us with any other ideas we had for bringing people in.'

MALCOLM: 'By then tourism had started. The first trickles were coming through but there was nothing much doing at that time except Nigel and Jenny Hinchliffe, who were doing their crockery and a few other bits and pieces.'

JENNY: 'Nigel and I had written a book together about Holmfirth, promoting the town and celebrating its history. There's a list of acknowledgements in it but

Kirklees Council doesn't feature. Nigel and I did it on our own with the help and support of people who lived in Holmfirth.'

BERYL: 'The council was more interested in promoting things going on in Dewsbury or Cleckheaton; districts that were generally more urban and poor, and it concentrated its efforts there to the detriment of the more rural areas.'

JACK: 'We once put plans in to put up a simple notice on the railings at the bottom of the road directing people to our shop. The people with businesses there said no problem, pop it on mate, but Kirklees refused permission. It was very frustrating.'

BERYL: 'But then at a Chamber of Trade meeting, one of our members stood up and said, "Do you know what I saw today? A coach full of visitors disembarking in the bus station. I asked them what they were all doing here, and they said, 'We've come to see where they film Last Of The Summer Wine." That's when we realised tourism was starting to be a big deal.'

JENNY: 'Nigel and I had become very friendly with Alan Bell and his wife, Connie. She would often come over with him and we went out for meals together a few times. We were having dinner one day and Alan said, "Do you think people would mind if, as part of the publicity for the show, we publicise Holmfirth itself? People are always saying it looks like a wonderful place and asking where it is." Nigel said, "What a good idea, I'm sure everyone here will be thrilled to bits." Well, he was wrong, wasn't he? There was a big article in the Radio Times about Holmfirth and Nigel was pictured in it showing off my pottery, and after that you've never seen anything like it. The trickle of tourists turned into a flood and a lot of locals hated it at first. People would shout things out when they were filming, spoiling the takes. The landlord of one of the pubs in the town was absolutely full of hate for the programme and the BBC. I never understood why. It was illogical to us. I realise it could be a bit of an inconvenience sometimes. There were times when you couldn't see the pavements for people. There were traffic jams everywhere and there was nowhere to park.

'But the show brought people to the town with money to spend. Coaches arrived from all over the country, sometimes three or four at a time. I can remember one day I'd done some Compo mugs and Nora Batty pin-up mugs, a gross of each so that's 288 mugs. I was just unpacking them in the shop and a coachload of women from Birmingham suddenly appeared outside. I knew that from their accents. Suddenly one of them called out: "Oi look, that's Bill Owen over there!" and then there was a stampede and Bill disappeared in a flurry of Brummies! They were crazy. It was like Beatlemania, and I could hear Bill's voice amongst them trying to calm them down. Eventually Nigel went out and rescued him and Bill emerged from the scrum looking a bit dishevelled. Then they all came in the shop and bought every single mug. Nothing left! I had to start again and order some more.'

Nigel Hinchliffe
(Jack Dunnill)

Stand-off!
(Malcolm Howarth)

JACK: 'Coachload after coachload of people started arriving. The drivers used to drop people off in the middle of Holmfirth, then go and park slightly out of town in the car park by the swimming pool at Sands.'

BERYL: 'It was really good for Holmfirth in so many different ways, yet there were people saying it wasn't the same "now that lot have come". Yes, there were times when it was a bit of a disruption. I remember one Bank Holiday Monday when I came to leave our shop and the pavements were so solid with people I could hardly get out. Sid's Cafe was a big draw and there were always visitors around Nora's steps.'

JACK: 'Bill Owen bought quite a lot of stuff from our antique shop and so did Kathy Staff, including some chairs, I recall. They'd pop in during breaks if they were filming. We did auctions too for years, and Bill would call in on the viewing days and say, "Jack, bid on this for me".'

JENNY: 'I liked Kathy very much. She was a lovely woman, and her husband was very pleasant as well. I went to their house once.'

BERYL: 'I put my foot in it on one occasion. In the antique shop we were plagued by visitors touching and handling things and all the time we were worried about items getting marked or damaged, so we were looking out all the time when people came into the shop. Once we had quite a few Hammond organs in and they were displayed near the entrance because they were so very heavy. Of course, people couldn't resist. "Ooh, look at that," they'd say, and start tinkling the ivories. We put a notice there, requesting Please Do Not Touch, which deterred a few potential concert pianists, but not all. One rainy day I was

in the office and I looked up just after three people had come in. They had their backs towards me with macs on and I could see them looking at one of the organs and pointing at it and I thought oh no, here we go. Then one of them reached his arm out and as soon as his fingers touched the keys, I shouted, "Can you leave that alone please!" He turned round and it was Brian Wilde, and Peter Sallis and Kathy Staff were there too. I said, "I'm sorry but we get so many people messing about with things." They were very nice about it.'

JACK: 'When Kirklees Council realised coachloads of people were coming to Holmfirth, they totally changed their tune. It changed their attitude completely and we found them much more cooperative.'

MALCOLM: 'The town became increasingly busy with tourists, coaches started coming and there was some resentment about that, even some business people who hadn't realised there was the potential there for them to make some serious money. Look at Holmfirth today – there are restaurants and cafes and an ice cream parlour. There was nothing like that. Lots of people could have taken advantage many years ago but didn't. Colin Frost bought Sid's Cafe and there was even some resentment from locals because it was a sort-of tourist attraction and somehow unseemly.'

JENNY: 'Slowly the anti-Summer Wine feeling among some of the other shopkeepers dissipated a bit. They opened up to it in the end, but they didn't like the fact we were so pally with people from the programme. A lot of them blamed Nigel for encouraging people to come to Holmfirth. That was daft. People wanted to come anyway. They would have found out, and some already had. Human beings can be a bit jealous, can't they? Nigel had become quite well known. He once got a postcard from a friend addressed simply to 'Nigel Hinchliffe, Mayor of Holmfirth.' Nothing else, no street name, let alone a postcode, and it reached him. In one of the programmes, Roy Clarke wrote the main characters some lines about Nigel Hinchliffe's nose. The BBC asked if I thought Nigel would mind and I said he'd be chuffed to bits. He pretended he wasn't, but he was. He thought it was wonderful. I designed a mug of him, and instead of a handle it had a nose.'

JACK: 'Bill Owen stayed with Nigel and Jenny up on the tops in Hade Edge. Very windswept. Bill and Nigel got on very well and you'd see them around together. Nigel, a big man with big, bushy hair, was very distinctive looking. You wouldn't confuse him with anyone else, or at least you wouldn't think so.'

JENNY: 'No you wouldn't, but I remember overhearing a woman saying, "Ooh Doris, we went out to Huddersfield on Saturday, to the George Hotel and you'll never guess who were there." "Who was it, Doris?" "It was that Scottish comedian Billy Connolly and his wife Pamela Stephenson, and they were with those old men off Last Of The Summer Wine." It had actually been me and Nigel, and Bill and Peter.'

ON LOCATION

MALCOLM: 'Filming on location is either all go or all stop, and a lot of the time it seems to be a lot more stop than go! Although if you look around, somebody is always doing something. You learn to ride with it. What are we waiting for? Well, it's the grips laying the track for the camera, or the props are being very carefully reset, or any one of a number of other things. There are a lot of tiny details that need taking care of, things you might not think of: wardrobe, make-up, and particularly matters concerning

View from Hade Edge
(Jenny Hinchliffe)

SUNDAY 2 SEPTEMBER

LOCATION BASE:	Nora Batty's area (Base as parking) (See Map L)
CONTACT:	Unit 'Phone: 0860 307250
PARKING:	Generator, lights, grips – Elephant and Castle Car Park. Winnebago, catering, ladies' caravan, toilets, costume/ make-up van – Fein's Mill Car Park. All other vehicles as directed by PM.
LOCATION:	Nora Batty's Rear of 28 Huddersfield Road Hollowgate Holmfirth
UNIT CALL:	0845 to set up. 0900 to turn over.
ARTISTS:	COMPO .... BILL OWEN CLEGG .... PETER SALLIS FOGGY .... BRIAN WILDE NORA .... KATHY STAFF
CALLS:	As arranged by AFM.
TRANSPORT:	1 Coach to leave Huddersfield Hotel at 0745. 2 Winnebago, toilets, ladies' caravan, costume/make-up van to be at location base by 0800.
CATERING:	Rolls available from 0830. Lunch 1245. Tea and coffee TBA.

Hollowgate, Holmfirth. The Elephant and Castle pub is seen to the right
(Jenny Hinchliffe)

continuity, so everything matches up when the scenes are edited in the cutting room. The continuity lady would be there with her pad, and there was always a set of polaroid pictures taken at the end of every scene so they didn't finish up with somebody with a hanky poking out of their pocket one moment, it disappearing the next, and then, oh dear, there it is back again at the end of the scene.

'I got to know the crew and what they all did, and we were all friends. My relationship with the actors tended to be more professional, though I'd sometimes chat with them at the catering wagon, especially at lunchtime. They weren't bad meals and I tried not to miss out. A decent, hot, three-course lunch and a table laid out with salad as well for you to help yourself. Peter Sallis impressed me as an actor. He was a very clever fella. Bill was brilliant on set in that he could switch from being Bill Owen to Compo and back again in a split second. You couldn't see any sign of Compo in his real life persona when he was out socially, dressed in his own smart togs, but on set, as soon as he put those scruffy clothes on, he could be Compo right on cue. Obviously, I couldn't go around distracting people by moving about and clicking the shutter during a take. Instead, it was up to me to step in quickly after a scene was completed and I'd ask the actors to hold their positions. I had read the script carefully first and picked out in my mind's eye what moments would make a good picture. Then I'd check the schedule and wait for things to unfold. Otherwise Alan Bell would jump in and say, "Right Malcolm, I want THAT photograph please." That would happen sometimes because I wouldn't always get a script. They could be like rocking horse droppings! 'The actors were generally fine with me, but I had a few problems with the crew. They'd be keen to get in there and strip everything down, the lighting guys especially. They weren't bothered about a photographer;

Location filming. All go or all stop!
(Malcolm Howarth)

they had a schedule to keep to and they had to get off to light the next set-up. To get round that, and to make sure I got the exposures I needed, I took my own reflectors and used flash. But it had to be instant, no messing about, because the actors needed to be away as well. "Have we done?" they'd say, "is that it?" And if you said, "No, just another one please," they'd sometimes get annoyed – even the really nice ones. I understood that. They were under pressure. They had a job to do. They had to check their schedules and run through their lines for their next scene. Sometimes it was freezing cold; they'd been standing around for an hour and they wanted to get inside and warm up. As the stills photographer I was an add-on to the crew and therefore, in some people's eyes, the least important technician out there. They appreciated the publicity before transmission when the filming was all over, but at the time they weren't best pleased. But I had a job to do as well and I had to stand up for myself. But there were people like Peter Sallis and Bill Owen who took a more rounded view. Their thinking was different. Bill would generally do anything to help. Even if he was a bit pushed for time or uptight, he'd say, "Alright, come on then, let's get it over with." And then he'd help me. "C'mon lads," he'd say to the sparks [electricians], "put that light back here will you, we haven't finished with it yet," and they jumped to it then. Bill could be my ally.

'Early on Alan Bell taught me a lesson I've never forgotten. It could be stressful on occasion, directing well-known actors, and there was a time when someone fobbed me off and I didn't get a good picture. I got a terrible shot that didn't capture the moment properly at all. "Look," Alan said, "you've got one chance to tell the story and there's no point you getting in there and taking any old picture and getting off. If you don't do it right, you don't do it at all. Stand your ground. Tell people exactly what you want them to do and don't take any

flannel." Those words were very wise. From then on, while remaining courteous and considerate, I stopped trying to rush and stood my ground, whoever they were. Brian Wilde could be an awkward customer. He'd puff and blow and say, "Oh no, no, no" but I'd politely insist and then, all of a sudden, as if by magic he'd change. "Do you mean like this?" "Yes, Brian, that's perfect." And from then on, he'd be fine. "Would you like another one Malcolm? How about if I stand like this?" Suddenly he was striking all sorts of poses in character and in the context of the scene and I'd get an excellent set of pictures. Once an actor realised that I knew what I was doing, everything would be fine, and everybody has been like that. If you pick up a camera and you're shy, dithering around with it, that's no good. Alan Bell was right. Go straight in and whether you're right or wrong, you direct the artist pleasantly, but firmly. "No, sorry, this is what I want..."

'I can usually see with my mind's eye what will work because as a press photographer I could be doing 15 different jobs a day. Some might be humdrum and boring, but you've got to know what will tell the story. I'd got that experience. Occasionally, as things unfold, once I've settled into the situation, I might see that it is not quite working as I hoped. But that's generally when I get a better idea, something that will work very well indeed, and I can start adjusting. "Right, can we try this one now..." and then you start getting a result that hits the mark perfectly and really tells the story. 'So you're covering up your mistakes and learning in the background, but when you've got that camera always let them know you know what you're doing, whether you actually do or not! You must have authority. You've got to control the situation, lay your stall out and stick to it. I've always remembered what Alan said that day and it's worked very well for me, also holding true for my press work. You can't settle for second best.'

"They used to call me he who disturbs no leaf!"
Foggy back in the jungle
(Malcolm Howarth)

LOOK AT THE LOVELY VIEW

Keen to exploit the visual charms of the Holme Valley to the very utmost, Alan Bell developed a great knowledge of the Holme Valley and its surroundings, setting out to find new locations for each series as well as returning to popular haunts. But as the years went on his task became harder. He wrote about the beginnings of all this in Jack Dunnill's 1988 Holmfirth Chamber of Trade souvenir publication, in a piece entitled The Day I Confounded Cleggy.

"I'm afraid we've filmed here before too." Peter Sallis gently reminded me – yet again – that it was pretty well impossible to find anywhere in the Holme Valley where Last Of The Summer Wine hadn't been before. I had just taken over the production in its sixth series. It was a particularly good summer that year (1981) and I really wanted to capture the atmosphere of Holmfirth itself, and the natural rugged beauty of the surrounding countryside that had so impressed me when I first arrived. And I wanted to find a new location too. Peter was right. They had been there before and I was shown the place where an inn called The Rising Sun had stood a year earlier before burning down on a night when the snow was so deep that the fire engines couldn't get through. Although nature was fast reclaiming the concrete foundations, the track which passed the inn soon revealed that a panoramic view of the valley had been thoughtfully placed for those who just want to sit and wonder what it must have been like when it was a prosperous woollen mill area.

We filmed several episodes there about metal detectors and car racing, and one where Compo was a phantom motorcyclist. But it was on that first day that Bill Owen, sensing my disappointment at not being the first BBC man at The Rising Sun, came over and, with all the confidentiality of a tipster giving me the winner of the Grand National, said, "Nigel Hinchliffe." "Who?" I asked. "Nigel Hinchliffe – go and see Nigel Hinchliffe. He'll sort out a new location for you." Nigel very kindly runs the corner shelter for those caught in the occasional Holme Valley shower. He also sells – strictly to pass the time of the visitor, I am told – newspapers and various souvenirs and artefacts, carefully imported from exotic, far-off countries. I was halfway through explaining that there were one or two locations I was having trouble finding when I found myself being driven at an alarming speed up hills, through forests and – I am sure – people's back gardens, all accompanied by a rapid-fire commentary.

That same summer, Michael Cager, our production manager, had found the ideal tin garage for a new character, Wesley Pegden

Holme Valley landscape
(Jean Shires)

(played by Gordon Wharmby), to tinker with that racing car, and a perfect nearby wall for Compo, Clegg and Foggy to observe. It hadn't been easy finding it and we had checked everything about it for backgrounds etc. On the morning that we arrived to film, we found some heavy earth-moving equipment had got there first and had removed our scenic background in readiness for a new housing development. As so often happens, the alternative home for Wesley, and later Edie (played by Thora Hird), which we found at Hinchliffe Mill was far better than the original. But yes, a sympathetic nod from Peter Sallis confirmed that they had filmed there before.

The two best-known locations for the series, the steps of Nora Batty and the cafe, now run by Ivy and Crusher (Jonathan Linsley) always bring back fond memories to me of two of the finest comedy actors I ever had the pleasure to work with – Joe Gladwin, who played Wally Batty, and John Comer, who played Ivy's husband Sid.

For most of us it will always be Sid's Cafe. It is interesting that when James Gilbert, the first producer, used the cafe it was a derelict fish and chip shop. When, in 1983 we made the first full-length film of the series, we installed the full interior of the cafe in order to film inside. From then on it stayed as a real cafe. Recently, for First Of The Summer Wine [a prequel to Last Of The Summer Wine], they temporarily changed it

back again into a fish and chip shop! It was the Gas Board who brought complete happiness to my life. On the day we were due to film a quiet scene in a lane not far from the White Horse at Jackson Bridge (just over the hill from Holmfirth), we found that the Gas Board had got there first and had already produced quite a large hole in the road with a pneumatic drill. There was absolutely no chance of doing any filming there that day.

Morale is all in filming, so I called the unit together. "Follow me in convoy, I know somewhere better." I didn't. I set off up the hill from the White Horse with the 20-odd trucks, coaches etc. following. Up the hill to the very top (which we now know to be Tinker's Tower), and then a sharp left into Intake Lane. It was as I turned left that I saw – too late – the No Through Road sign. I kept going with the convoy crowding in behind until we arrived at the inevitable end of the road. There it was. The most perfect location we had used, heather-clad lanes and a quite spectacular view of New Mill below. So good was the location that we have used it for almost every episode since Peter Sallis took in the view and said, "Well, I must say we've never been here before – how did you find it?" "Well," I replied, savouring my satisfaction, "it sort of came to me." We resolved to keep the location secret and we haven't let on to anyone since.

Chapter Six

FROM SHAKESPEARE AND MUSIC HALL

How do you replace a character like Foggy Dewhurst? Roy Clarke came up with Seymour, another old school chum of Compo and Clegg, who first appeared as, and in, Uncle Of The Bride, a special episode broadcast on New Year's Day 1986. Unlike his illustrious ex-army predecessors, Seymour Utterthwaite was not a former military man. Instead, he was the former headmaster of a minor public school for boys, and in his mind at least, something of an aristocrat. Seymour was, to a degree, a gentleman. He certainly sounded posh and without doubt he thought himself a cut above Compo and Clegg. Moreover, he was given to lecturing those around him, as teachers often do. Something of an absent-minded, nutty professor, Seymour was an inveterate amateur inventor and although catastrophe-prone, he remained utterly convinced that recognition of his inventive genius was imminent and long overdue. Continuing the show's third man tradition, he was quite barmy.

A new chapter: Clegg, Seymour, and Compo
(Malcolm Howarth)

Seymour Utterthwaite surveys his territory
(Malcolm Howarth)

Alan Bell chose distinguished theatre actor Michael Aldridge for the role, and Clarke tailored the part for him. Aldridge, though well-known in the theatre world, was not entirely familiar to television audiences. A doctor's son, born in Somerset in 1920, he was determined to be an actor as a schoolboy and made his professional debut while still a teenager. Inevitably, the Second World War interrupted his career plans and Aldridge served in the RAF as an air gunner and navigator. Once demobbed, he joined the Old Vic, where roles included Othello and MacBeth. He then moved into musical comedy, played the Chichester Festival and in the West End, joined the RSC, was cast in farces, and performed in plays by the Alans, Ayckbourn and Bennett. Television work included Tinker Tailor Soldier Spy, and a title role as a buffoonish clot, Caldicott in Keith Waterhouse's comedy drama 'Charters

and Caldicott'. A big man, Aldridge stood at six feet four inches. He was well spoken and clearly well-educated with a fruity, expressive voice, and he had a natural, if slightly shabby, dignity. He was minor theatrical royalty, and his acting persona carried weight and authority, exuding a sort of weathered benevolence.

Aldridge's comic timing was exquisite, and his gravitas made Seymour's daftness all the more bonkers. Uncle of the Bride featured Seymour's niece, Glenda, marrying her fiancé Barry. These parts were played by Sarah Thomas and Mike Grady, and there was a guest appearance by veteran actress Dame Thora Hird as Seymour's sister Edie, Glenda's mother and wife of Wesley Pegden, a Fred Dibdah-esque amateur car mechanic who had already made a one-off appearance back in series six. Wesley was played by Gordon Wharmby.

All smiles before departure but the car was less than fully confidence-inspiring!
(Malcolm Howarth)

Don't mind if I do. Mother and daughter Edie and Glenda fitting in nicely
(Malcolm Howarth)

Wesley seems a trifle concerned
(Malcolm Howarth)

Barry and Glenda
(Malcolm Howarth)

Crusher eating the profits
(Malcolm Howarth)

Gordon Wharmby was a painter and decorator, and part-time actor from Manchester who struck it lucky when Bell cast him as Wesley in his first series as the show's director. Wharmby was called to audition for a one-line part, but so impressed Bell that he was asked to stay on and read for Wesley Pegden. A down-to-earth, working man in real life, Wharmby brought authenticity to Wesley's character. Roy Clarke liked what he saw and later incorporated Wesley as a series regular. Edie and Wesley's daughter Glenda was another new character first introduced in Uncle of the Bride. Actress Sarah Thomas had extensive television experience including appearing in Worzel Gummidge with Jon Pertwee, but she was picked by Bell after he saw her performing on stage near his Surrey home.

Considered naive by the other women in her mother's coffee circle, even years later when she was middle-aged, Glenda had a gentle nature, but she could, on occasion, be a force to be reckoned with. Her views were often dismissed by her mother ("Drink your coffee!") but she would occasionally defend the show's hapless menfolk. Although she loved her husband, Barry, she could sometimes be dissatisfied with her lot.

Barry Wilkinson was meek, harmless and a trifle humdrum. An office-bound clerk, he dreamed of a more interesting and exciting life but routine and domesticity would remain his lot despite attempting various new hobbies to broaden his horizons. Terrified of his domineering mother-in-law, he was anxious to keep his modern motor car out of his father-in-law's tinkering hands.

Mike Grady was hand-picked by Bell to play Barry. Trained at the Bristol Old Vic, Grady had extensive stage experience and had appeared in high-profile films including The Return of the Pink Panther. But he was perhaps best known for playing Ken, sidekick to

Robert Lindsay's Wolfie, in the hugely successful 1970s sitcom Citizen Smith. There would be other new characters too due to the extended fall-out from Wilde's departure, as Roy Clarke changed to a more ensemble approach for the show's stories; keeping to the idea of having three men at the show's heart, but bringing in more characters around them with which to build storylines. A stage play based on the programme played to reasonable reviews and happy audiences in London and Eastbourne in 1983, and in Bournemouth the following summer. A pacy, chaotic farce, it featured Bill Owen and Peter Sallis, both of whom were excellent, and Jane Freeman, but not Brian Wilde. Foggy had been confined to bed with a bad back, according to the script, and he was heard banging his stick from his bedroom offstage.

For this play Clarke wrote several new characters: Ivy gained a strapping nephew, Crusher, to help her in the cafe; a peroxide forty-something floosie called Marina developed a romantic crush on Norman Clegg; and a new middle-aged married couple, Howard and Pearl Sibshaw. The first run featured Huddersfield-born actor Kenneth Waller, later to find fame as Grandad in Carla Lane sitcom Bread, as Howard. Alan Bell and Clarke saw the show together in Bournemouth during its second year and, impressed by the actors playing the newcomers, sensed new opportunities. After the performance Peter Sallis and Bill Owen were dispatched to talk to them and subsequently their characters, the large and intimidating, but ultimately harmless Crusher; the blowsy blonde Marina; and the quarrelling Sibshaws, would all soon be incorporated into the series itself.

Jean Fergusson, who played Marina, was born not far from Summer Wine Land in Woolley near Wakefield but her family moved away, and she eventually completed her education at Bridgend in

An unlikely Romeo: Robert Fyfe
(Malcolm Howarth)

Wales. After starting on stage in am-dram, she later trained professionally. In Waller's shoes as Howard was Alloa-born Robert Fyfe, who studied drama in Bradford. Juliette Kaplan was Pearl Sibshaw, in place of Jean Trend. Originally from Bournemouth, Kaplan owned gift shops in the town but was much travelled and had lived for a time as a child in New York City. In years to come Kaplan appeared as Pearl in a one-woman touring show written for her by Clarke.

In the television series the subject of Marina's romantic intentions would be Howard Sibshaw, although there would be occasional oblique references to her having had a past liaison with Clegg, to his obvious great discomfort. Marina was a tarty former glamour girl, an unmarried woman of a certain age desperate for love and romance – so desperate, in fact, that she'd fall for Howard, though occasionally giving up on him temporarily and falling for other unsuitable men. Many of Clarke's male characters could be described as henpecked, and dapper tank-topped bicyclist Howard especially so. Timid, weasel-faced, flat capped, and ageing, he was the most unlikely Romeo. Nonetheless he dreamed of escaping from his somehow all-seeing, waspish wife. Forever plotting, Howard would come up with myriad sneaky schemes involving umpteen crazy locations for secret liaisons with the sensuous Marina, all of which would inevitably go terribly, and embarrassingly wrong.

Always one step ahead of Howard's devious schemes, gimlet-eyed Pearl would bide her time, waiting with pursed lips and folded arms, holding her acid tongue until Howard and Marina's flawed plans went disastrously awry. Sour and censorious, Pearl was a fearsome female of the species like no other in Summer Wine Land.

Romance in store. Jean Fergusson
(Malcolm Howarth)

The wrath of Pearl. Juliette Kaplan and Robert Fyfe
(Malcolm Howarth)

Howard and Marina, thwarted time and time again
(Malcolm Howarth)

Poor Marina was particularly long-suffering, having to cope with the disapproval of the series' other battle-axes as well as the withering wrath of Pearl, and tolerate the altogether feeble efforts of her moustachioed would-be paramour. There was something of the

```
"LAST OF THE SUMMER WINE"  -  SERIES Q - EPISODE ONE


Artist                   Character


BILL OWEN                Compo               FILM/STAGES
PETER SALLIS             Clegg               FILM/STAGES
BRIAN WILDE              Foggy               FILM/STAGES
KATHY STAFF              Nora Batty          FILM/STAGES
JANE FREEMAN             Ivy                 FILM/STAGES
THORA HIRD               Edie                STAGES
ROBERT FYFE              Howard              FILM/STAGES
JULIETTE KAPLAN          Pearl               STAGES
JEAN FERGUSSON           Marina              FILM
SARAH THOMAS             Glenda              STAGES
DANNY O'DEA              Eli                 FILM
                        Traffic Warden       FILM
                        Landlord             FILM
                        P.C.                 FILM
                        Policeman            FILM
                        Protest Man          FILM


ROBIN BANKS             Compo Double         FILM
DENNIS MAWN            Clegg Double          FILM
TONY SIMON             Foggy Double          FILM




SUPPORTING ARTISTS


FILM

Barmaid
Pub customers
Protestors
```

A fallen woman
(Malcolm Howarth)

Bamforth postcard about peroxided Marina as she tottered about in high heels, a short skirt and bulging blouse, and she remained strangely dignified, even as everything inevitably fell apart, somehow remaining optimistic despite countless crushing disappointments.

Howard too was an eternal optimist, and while he and Marina hurried and scurried and plotted and hid, they were more childlike than raunchy in their naughtiness. They were essentially innocents whose relationship was to remain forever chaste, and the audience's gusty laughter lay in their being thwarted time and again, and in anticipation of it.

A NEW DIMENSION
Uncle Of The Bride drew an audience of 18.1 million but the critics missed Foggy and were not so sure about the show's new look. Another seasonal special was transmitted at the end of 1986, followed by 12 new episodes in early 1987; effectively a double series to firmly establish Seymour. Edie Pegden featured in a couple of episodes in series nine and then became a fixture, and Barry and Glenda, and Howard, Marina and Pearl also settled in during its run. Edie and Wesley honed their hilarious newspaper routine, with Edie flashing printed pages into place with split-second timing to protect her carpets, walls, and woodwork from Wesley's oily extremities. Thora Hird developed Edie's eccentric persona, drawing on her own Auntie Nellie as she adopted airs and graces and a plummy, pretend-posh voice. Determined to be a cut above and striving for social superiority, she'd twitch in discomfort if Glenda or Wesley appeared too common in company. Roy Clarke liked having more options. Introducing so many supporting characters and nutty inventor Seymour Utterthwaite at the same time brought a new dimension to the show,

and he wrote even more slapstick and madcap adventures into his scripts. With yet more visual comedy, the programme became more family friendly than ever.

These episodes featured crazy, weird and outlandish inventions. There were more stunts and zany adventures and fewer talking heads. Alan Bell made more use of stunt men and body doubles, but Bill Owen's clowning brilliance certainly helped bring off this change. Still game in his seventies, he was regularly up for physical gags; for climbing, running, jumping, falling, for getting drenched with water. Just William at 70 as he saw it, forever the schoolboy. Owen was paraphrasing a little more now but would still take to his caravan to check who had the most lines. And for all the visual humour, Clarke's dialogue remained razor sharp.

RIGHT: Still game. Bill Owen was always up for physical humour
(Malcolm Howarth)

SCENE 5 – FILM: EXT. STREET. DAY 1.

COMPO IS WALKING ALONG QUITE
CHEERFULLY UNTIL HE BEGINS TO
FEEL THE PRESENCE OF A STONE
IN HIS WELLIE.

HE LIMPS ALONG FOR A WHILE
OCCASIONALLY PAUSING TO SHAKE
HIS FOOT TO TRY AND REARRANGE
THE THING.

THIS NOT BEING SUCCESSFUL HE
SITS DOWN ON EITHER A LOW WALL
OR A BENCH AND REMOVES HIS WELLIE.

NOTHING FALLS OUT WHEN HE SHAKES
IT. HE RAISES THE WELLIE HIGH
IN THE AIR AND BEGINS TO PEER
UP INSIDE THE WELLIE AND HE'S
IN THIS POSITION WHEN ELI PASSES.

ELI WALKS ROUND COMPO STARING
UP AT THE WELLIE IN SOME
ADMIRATION.

ELI SHAKES HIS HEAD.

ELI
I don't know how anybody can get

their leg that high without doing

terrible damage.

One of Seymour's many crazy inventions
(Malcolm Howarth)

Veteran music hall comedian and panto dame Danny O'Dea first appeared in series nine playing Eli Duckett, an elderly friend of Wally Batty, in an episode entitled Jaws. A complete crackpot and as blind as a bat, Eli caused panic and chaos playing darts in the White Horse pub. Eli made cameo appearances for some time afterwards, sometimes on a bicycle, but O'Dea had difficulty following direction and Bell found him exasperatingly hard work. Nonetheless, Eli became a firm fans' favourite and composer Ronnie Hazlehurst delighted in writing special pieces of music to underscore his

Ronnie Hazlehurst
(Malcolm Howarth)

hilarious appearances.

On occasion, Hazlehurst also wrote comic pastiches of famous and popular TV and movie themes, such as Dallas and ET, cleverly and appropriately blending them with the show's score. By now Hazlehurst's music was as much part of the show as Compo, Clegg or Nora Batty, and the programme's haunting theme tune was instantly recognisable by millions worldwide thanks to its audiences in Australia, New Zealand, Canada, and the United States.

TAKING ADVANTAGE

Like many people in Holmfirth, the real resident of Nora Batty's house, Sonia Lee, had an excellent relationship with the Summer Wine cast and crew. But there remained a degree of disgruntlement among some citizens in the town, and there were a few examples of opportunistic greed. People started demanding inconvenience money, forcing Alan Bell to move Cleggy's and Howard's houses to an alternative location. Noisy builders near Nora's wanted a chunk of cash to shut up and go away, and an obnoxious neighbour near number 28 Huddersfield Road almost forced Nora out, with Bell going as far as to film her house with a sold sign outside as Nora made a final trip down her famous steps. Fortunately, the sequence was never used.

BERYL DUNNILL: 'Not everybody was helpful to the BBC. There was one young woman in particular who caused problems.'

On Nora's steps
(Malcolm Howarth)

JENNY HINCHLIFFE: 'Yes, I know who you mean. She was horrid, and always eating. "All the boys are after me, you know," she'd say. "They all want to kiss me".'

BERYL: 'She had children very young and went to live near Nora Batty's house where she came up with a plan to make some money. As soon as the BBC turned up and started filming on the steps, she opened all the windows, set the dog off barking, wound the kids up to make as much noise as possible and played records as loudly as she could. When someone from the crew asked her to keep the noise down, she held her hand out – "Money please".'

MALCOLM HOWARTH: 'For a while it was the same every year. Windows wide open, and loud music on the record player. Ooh, she was an obnoxious young lady. She knew the BBC was committed to filming there so would do the best she could to make it difficult until they gave her something. In the end they used to pay for her to go on holiday for a week so they could film at Nora's. I knew her parents a bit and felt sorry for them. She was an embarrassment.'

Script pages from Last Of The Summer Wine.
Interpretation by Jenny Hinchliffe

SCENE 2 - FILM: EXT. NORA'S.
DAY 1.

NORA IS FINISHING HANGING OUT
HER LINE OF WASHING. SHE STEPS
BACK TO ADMIRE HER HANDIWORK.
IT REALLY IS A LINE OF VERY NICE
CLEAN WASHING. SHE GIVES A SMALL
NOD OF SATISFACTION AND GOES
BACK UP THE STEPS INTO HER HOUSE.

COMPO WHO HAS BEEN WATCHING
TIPTOES HURRIEDLY UP HIS STEPS,
CROSSES TO NORA'S CLOTHES LINE,
PULLS A BUNDLE OUT FROM UNDER
HIS JACKET AND PEGS IT ONTO THE
END OF NORA'S CLOTHES LINE.

IT'S A PAIR OF HIS COMBINATIONS
WHICH HE WANTS TO DRY. THEY ARE
IN MARKED CONTRAST TO THE REST
OF THE WASHING ON THE LINE.

COMPO SNEAKS BACK DOWN HIS STEPS.

WE SEE NORA'S SHOCKED FACE
APPEAR AT THE WINDOW. SHE HURRIES
OUTSIDE FOR A CLOSER LOOK AT WHAT'S
HAPPENED.

SHE STORMS DOWN HER STEPS AND
COMPO'S STEPS AND HAULS HIM BACK
UP THE STEPS.

COMPO
Steady on lass, tha's got a grip

like a python.

NORA
Get them things off. Suppose

somebody passes and thinks that's my

standard of washing.

COMPO
I think it goes deeper than that.

I think it sets thee blood racing

seeing my long johns on your

widowed clothes line.

NORA
I've told you before about hanging

things on my clothes line.

COMPO
I've nowhere to hang 'em.

NORA
They want burning. They're past

washing. I've told you before, why

do you keep doing it?

COMPO BEGINS REMOVING THE GARMENT.

COMPO
I think psychologically I'm just

marking me territory.

HE DODGES HER SWIPE AND GOES
GIGGLING BACK TO HIS PLACE.

CUT TO EXT. STREET.   FILM.

A CASE OF MISTAKEN IDENTITY

Filming went well on series nine, apart from Bell having to use a stand-in to get around the absence of a key character. Gifted amateur actor Gordon Wharmby had become highly stressed about being paired with Thora Hird, finding the prospect of playing the husband of such a famous woman completely overwhelming.

MALCOLM: 'Gordon Wharmby was a nice bloke. He had a serious wobble, and I was there the night it happened. A few of us were chatting in the White Horse and he became hyperactive, trying to impress, talking far too much and getting really agitated. I remember thinking there's something wrong here, calm down Gordon. Other people noticed it too. Then he went too far and created a bit of a disturbance and the next day he was taken away to hospital. And of course, some big gob in the pub told someone who contacted the papers, and the following morning there was knocking at the door of the White Horse. The poor guy was ill, obviously. How the papers were going to handle the story, goodness knows. Ron Backhouse [the landlord] phoned and said, "I've got Fleet Street reporters here Malcolm, banging on my door. Where are you? They're telling me that Brian Wilde has had a breakdown, started throwing furniture about in the pub, and had to go off to hospital." They'd got it wrong – got the wrong guy. "Oh, alright Ron," I said, cottoning on. I shot down to the pub, got these reporters in tow and took them to where the cast and crew were on location at Sid's Cafe in Holmfirth. Alan Bell had been warned and everyone totally ignored the reporters I had with me. None of the crew took any notice of them at all. I said, "These guys have heard that Brian's not so well." "Oh," said Alan, "Perhaps they'd like to stay a few minutes and see him in this scene that we're shooting." Well, Brian was right on the top of his game, and after a while the journalists all sloped off. They never clicked on the story was about somebody else. It never occurred to them they'd got the wrong man. We pulled the wool over their eyes and got away with it. Of course, it all came out later, but by then Gordon was well again and it was yesterday's news.'

After a personal visit from Bell, Gordon Wharmby agreed to return to the cast for the wedding scenes in Uncle Of The Bride. He was fragile at first but did well and gradually regained confidence.

MORE INS AND OUTS

Joe Gladwin died in March 1987 and thereafter Nora would have more scenes with fellow on-screen widow and long-time friend and partner-in-arms, Ivy. Edie began hosting the ladies' gossip group, a popular fixture in the programme, and frequent outings in Edie's terrifying Triumph Herald gave the wardrobe department irresistible opportunities for experimentation with dreadful hat and coat combinations for Holmfirth's most famous female resident, she of the wrinkled stockings.

Gordon Wharmby and his on-screen wife, Dame Thora Hird
(Malcolm Howarth)

By now special episodes were an expected component of the BBC's Christmas holiday schedule, and on December 27, 1987, Big Day At Dream Acres featured distinguished Irish actor Ray McAnally playing a wily tramp. Series ten would be broadcast during October and November the following year with a further Christmas Special, entitled Crums, transmitted on Christmas Eve 1988, and featuring a very special new character. Howard's Auntie Wainwright soon became a regular in what was now a more ensemble cast than ever. The money-grabbing junk shop owner was played by Jean Alexander, another inspired suggestion by Alan Bell's wife, Constance.

Series ten had already featured former sitcom star Stephen Lewis as Smiler. Tall, miserable and gormless, ex-army man Smiler came into the series as Nora Batty's lodger, much to Compo's chagrin. He wore a flat cap and old-fashioned overcoat, and first appeared as a lollipop man before working in Auntie Wainwright's shop. Stephen Lewis was a lugubrious Londoner hugely famous for playing Blakey, the bus inspector in the early 1970s sitcom On The Buses, and in spin-off feature films from the series.

Wally Batty, central in this photo and in Nora's life. After Joe Gladwin died in 1987, Nora never remarried.
(Malcolm Howarth)

Lewis worked in construction and served in the Merchant Navy before discovering acting through joining Joan Littlewood's experimental Theatre Workshop in the 1950s. He was also an accomplished playwright and director.

MALCOLM: 'Stephen Lewis was a lovely fella. A genuine person. The public would often approach him as though he were Blakey in On The Buses and he didn't mind a bit. He'd fall into character dead easy. And he wouldn't just pose, pull a face, he'd actually become Blakey and do a bit. "I'll get you for this, Butler!" He'd do it for me too, to help him get the right faces for my pictures, which made it easy and fun.

A national treasure: Jean Alexander as Auntie Wainwright
(Malcolm Howarth)

"I'll get you for this, Butler!" Off duty, Stephen Lewis was happy to reprise his famous character, Blakey from On the Buses
(Malcolm Howarth)

Smiler in the wars
(Malcolm Howarth)

Drag racing! All a crazy ruse to make Marina jealous

(Malcolm Howarth)

A greedy and unscrupulous woman
(Malcolm Howarth)

'Some time after he joined Summer Wine there was an episode where Smiler and Barry dressed up as women and let Howard drive them around in a car. It was all a ruse to make Marina jealous because she reckoned she'd gone off men. Burnlee Club car park was the base on that particular day, the place where Barry Took had filmed before the series had even started, because the bulk of the shooting was taking place at Wesley and Edie's in Hinchliffe Mill, just up the road. They were fetching the artists from the caravans as they needed them, and Stephen had been ready for some time, dressed as a woman, looking grotesque and utterly ridiculous in a wig and make up, waiting to be collected for his scenes in the car.

'It gets a bit boring on set. They can be two or three hours on a scene. I wasn't needed so I wandered back to the base where there'd always be cups of tea and coffee, and I could chat to whoever was about. Obviously, Stephen was bored too because he started putting on a show, standing at the roadside waving to people driving by in cars dressed as this hideous woman. Somebody took offence and reported it to the police. It was all smoothed over, but it would have made a lovely news story.'

Auntie Wainwright was a greedy and unscrupulous woman feared by the men in the series, especially Clegg. She appeared to be a harmless old lady, but was sneaky and mean, and scurried back and forth slyly selling utterly useless objects to anyone she lured into her shop. Whining and tremulous of voice, she pretended to be cheated if she ever gave the slightest discount.

She kept a gun, and when customers entered her premises of their own free will, Auntie Wainwright would terrify them by using a loudhailer to make deafening announcements such as, "Stay where you are! Don't touch anything or you will be electrocuted!" Jean Alexander was born in Toxteth, Liverpool in 1926 and after a grounding in rep became famous and greatly loved for playing gossipy cleaning lady Hilda Ogden in northern soap opera Coronation Street. After 23 years she left The Street to national dismay, saying she was taking a career break, but would come back to acting if the right scripts came along. An expert comedy actress, Alexander was a long-standing admirer of Clarke's work and had always wanted to play what she described as "a prickly character". The beady-eyed Auntie Wainwright gave her a perfect opportunity to realise that ambition and, like Thora Hird before her, she brought a great deal of audience

goodwill with her when she joined the show. Both women were also popular with the crew, Alexander in particular.

BREAKFAST WITH JEAN

MALCOLM: 'You couldn't wish for a nicer person than Jean Alexander. Every year I went to London for around three days to cover the studio sessions. I'd look at the schedule and pick out the best days so I could maximise my time and photograph the majority of the cast in costume on the interior sets. One year at Shepperton Studios a young reporter arrived from the Huddersfield Examiner. She was new and a bit nervous. I took her onto the set to see Jean and asked her if she'd mind doing an interview with this young lady. "Oh yes," said Jean straight away, and I was expecting to find them a quiet corner somewhere for ten minutes, but then Jean said, "I'm staying over the other side of the square from you, aren't I?" She was absolutely right. The reporter's hotel on Church Square in Shepperton was just across from Jean's. They were sister hotels. "I'll tell you what," she said, "I'll come over to yours tomorrow morning and we'll sit by the river."

'Well, the next morning we all finished up having breakfast together by the Thames and the young reporter got an interview which lasted from nine o'clock

On location in the Colne Valley
(Malcolm Howarth)

until half past twelve. It was a lovely, informal chat and afterwards Jean said, "I really enjoyed that. I'm off home now." She hadn't even needed to have stayed in London that morning, let alone given us so much of her time.

You'd get other people looking at their watch, saying, "I have to be off," or "you've got enough now," that kind of thing, but not Jean. "Shall we have toasted teacakes?" she said at one point. And when she ordered them, she said to the waiter, "Put them on my bill." She was such a lovely lady.'

CRUSHER

Crusher was played by Jonathan Linsley, who trained at Bristol Old Vic and made numerous film, theatre and television appearances before and after his stint on Summer Wine, not least as Ogilvey in two 'Pirates of the Caribbean' films. He is also a talented artist.

The character of Crusher was quietly dropped, for reasons Jack and Beryl Dunnill explain.

JACK: 'Once the cast and crew finished for the day, they were sometimes stuck for things to do. Bill Owen would occasionally pop in to see us at the pub. Peter Sallis preferred to relax in his hotel and have a few glasses of wine over dinner, I understand. He didn't stay in Holmfirth, but Bill and some of the others did. It made sense in many ways.'

BERYL: 'When he was Crusher, Jonathan Linsley used to enjoy socialising with us and other members of the Chamber of Trade, and soon after he left the series he came to Holmfirth with his wife for old times' sake and booked in for the weekend at the Old Bridge Hotel.'

JACK: 'He rang us up. "Jack," he said, "can you get the old gang together? Let's have a night out." I made a few phone calls and arranged to meet him in the bar at the Old Bridge. But when we got there, he was nowhere to be seen. I looked everywhere. Then I saw someone waving and saying, "Jack, it's me, I'm over here." He'd lost such a huge amount of weight that I literally hadn't recognised him. That's why he lost his job on Summer Wine. He was written out because he was no longer a formidably big guy. He no longer suited the part and his days in the programme were done.'

BERYL: 'He'd been warned health-wise that he needed to lose the weight, so what else could he do?'

JACK: 'Of course. But anyway, we all had a great weekend together; Jonathan and his wife, Nigel and Jenny, Beryl and me and the rest of the Chamber of Trade gang, and we're still in touch with Jonathan today.'

Out on his ear
(Malcolm Howarth)

Night shoot at Auntie Wainwright's
(Malcolm Howarth)

Memories of Seymour

Greatly liked by all who worked with him, Michael Aldridge was Seymour Utterthwaite from January 1986 to September 1990
(Malcolm Howarth)

Leading men. Writer Roy Clarke with Peter Sallis, Michael Aldridge and Bill Owen outside the White Horse pub in Jackson Bridge
(Malcolm Howarth)

A HAPPY SHIP

Michael Aldridge was a kind, good natured and caring man who was good to work with. Outgoing, gregarious, and full of joie de vivre, he made an effort to learn the crew's names from day one and encouraged socialising among the cast. Aldridge was good company, ebullient and full of stories. He got on especially well with Peter Sallis with whom he would regularly have dinner at the Huddersfield Hotel, and the pair often dined out together, sometimes persuading others to join them. Even Bill Owen occasionally broke his routine to meet them at a restaurant.

The women in the cast also enjoyed each other's company during evenings at the Huddersfield Hotel; although Thora Hird liked to be the centre of attention, and as the years rolled on she tended to dominate the dinnertime conversation, talking across the top of people, sometimes a little boastfully. And as can sometimes be the case as people grow older, she became increasingly prone to repetition. Sallis in particular came to be a little irritated by her. But Hird was essentially a kind and generous person, and pleasant enough to be with one to one, and she and Sarah Thomas became increasingly close, their relationship developing almost as if they really were mother and daughter. The veteran actress was very fond of her on-screen offspring, and in the tiredness of evening, fiction and real life became blurred.

Hird was never happier than when she was recognised by the public. On her days off she liked being out and about in Huddersfield, particularly in the town's covered market. When she travelled to and from London by train the BBC always provided a first-class ticket, but she preferred to sit in a second-class coach to be among people with whom she could enjoy a friendly chat.

Jean Alexander, on the other hand, was more reserved, and happy to remain incognito, but she always had time for people who recognised her.

MALCOLM: 'Jean could switch Hilda Ogden on straight away if she felt like it. If she was pushed, she'd do it to please people, although she would never volunteer it.'

On location the leading men co-existed without friction, and the women would congregate in Thora's caravan, talking and laughing and playing cards. Michael Aldridge had made a difference. By force of his personality, and at his insistence, everybody in the cast and crew got along very well indeed. Whether on location or relaxing in the evening, during the late 1980s the Last Of The Summer Wine ship was, overall, a very happy one.

Edie comforts her on-screen daughter, Glenda. Dame Thora was very fond of Sarah Thomas in real life
(Malcolm Howarth)

Pearl, Edie and Glenda appraise the goods, while Auntie Wainwright is anxious to close the deal
(Malcolm Howarth)

Outside Auntie Wainwright's
(Malcolm Howarth)

The smiles are genuine. In the late 1980s Last Of The Summer Wine was a happy show
(Malcolm Howarth)

Chapter Seven

BEHIND THE SCENES

By now Malcolm Howarth was an established member of the crew, on hand to observe the show's new stars settling in.

MALCOLM: 'Michael Aldridge was a really nice fella. He was educated and well spoken, but he'd speak to you properly and normally whatever your station in life. He wouldn't speak down to anyone at all, which is something you might not expect if you saw his character. In real life he was on the same level as the rest of us, but when he was acting, he became someone on an entirely different level. Oh yes, he was something else again – one above. He was a classical actor and that emanated from every pore. It made Seymour, his character, look a complete idiot, which was very clever of Roy Clarke. Michael giving forth in that Shakespearean way of his suited Seymour really well.

'Robert Fyfe is a timid man, a bit like he is as Howard in the programme. He's a very friendly guy who always had the time to speak to you at lunch or between scenes, but after the day's work was done, he was his own person, and he was away. He was quite private, and you wouldn't see him out for a drink with the crew.

'Jean Fergusson was full of herself but in a good way. She was a bubbly, bouncy, extrovert character; a really nice, fun-loving person, but not in a flirty way at all like Marina. She turned up for work one day on a motorbike, I recall! Jean could do a fantastic impression of Hylda Baker – "She knows, you know. Ooh, I'm overcome with emotion" – absolutely terrific, which is comical when you compare the size of the two women. Jean was tall and Hylda was tiny. She wrote a biography of Hylda Baker and also a one woman tribute show about her which Jean starred in and took on tour. I went to watch her perform it in Oldham and she was absolutely brilliant. We went backstage afterwards and Jean took us onto the stage to see the set. We hadn't realised the furniture was enormous, specially built so Jean would look small. The chair she'd been sitting on was huge and so was the bed.

'Juliette Kaplan could be a bit sharp-tongued on occasion, but she always turned in a very professional and polished performance, and if you matched her in that respect, she'd have every respect for you. I knew that with Juliette I had to be firm, no messing about. "I'd like you to sit there please, like that, and give me the expression on your face please from just here in the script." If you were definite about what you wanted, you'd be ok. But if you dithered at all, she'd sometimes have something to say. Mike Grady is a really good bloke. He'd join in just like a local and Sarah Thomas was the same. They were both quiet people and reserved at first, but once Mike got warmed up, he could be quite amusing.

"Thora Hird had been a huge star in her time, and you could still sense it. But she was a very nice person and lovely to work with. She'd never pull you down.

Howard and Marina: "I think we've cracked it this time!"
(Malcolm Howarth)

Put a ring on it! Glenda and Barry
(Malcolm Howarth)

Cheers! Edie Pegden
(Malcolm Howarth)

When I'd say, "Can I get a picture please?" there were some who'd groan and make it clear they didn't want you there, especially the extras. They were the worst. Superstars they were! But I don't think I ever heard Thora complain about anything or say a bad word about anyone. Having said that, she didn't like swearing around her. She wouldn't have it. She was a genuine Christian in the wrong trade because she must have come across some right spivs and wheeler-dealers over the years in the entertainment business!

Once we were filming outside Edie's house in Hinchliffe Mill on a lovely, red hot day, but then black clouds came rolling over and it started raining heavily. The brollies came out but then hailstones started pelting down. When that sort of thing happened, we were all in it together and did anything we could to help get the equipment under cover. I just had a camera around my neck, so I helped too. Everybody was dashing hither and thither, and we finally dived for cover ourselves. But poor Thora was pretty much immobile. She was stuck in her chair and there was no time to get her to safety. All we could do was prop up some of the umbrellas to protect her the best we could. Afterwards I went to see if she was alright. She was fine. She didn't let that sort of thing bother her. Then I noticed she was looking at something intently. There was a little flower border nearby with some beautiful tall flowers in it like delphiniums. Tall stems with lots of little flowers like trumpets. On one of these plants the trumpets had filled with water and the weight had kinked the stem and taken it down in the hail. "Malcolm," she said, "will you do me a favour? Will you stand that flower up and tie it to that stick?" Then she got one of the make-up girls to go and fetch some string for me. She caught my attention again a bit later and she said, "Thank you very much for doing that Malcolm, there's a couple of weeks of pleasure left in that flower for somebody." Little things like that stick in your mind.'

FIRST OF THE SUMMER WINE

Set in 1939 and featuring a youthful Compo, Clegg, Foggy and Seymour, First Of The Summer Wine was a clever prequel to the main show which ran for two series in 1988 and 1989. Alan Bell was not chosen to direct. Instead, BBC Head of Comedy Gareth Gwenlan took responsibility for the pilot episode with Mike Stephens taking the helm thereafter, and Ronnie Hazlehurst was not asked to provide a score, with period music being used throughout. The wartime setting was nostalgic for older viewers and the characters got involved in similar escapades to their older selves, with Peter Sallis adding a degree of continuity and familiarity by appearing as Norman Clegg's father.

There were high hopes for the series, not least in the mind of Roy Clarke who had ambitious plans to develop the concept further. But perhaps it was just not as funny watching young lads behaving in a childlike manner as it was older men, and the programme somehow lacked the charm of the original. Sadly, the show never really took off in terms of audience ratings. There is a theory among insiders that the BBC baulked at funding a third series in the hope of growing an audience because the show's budget was too high, a fortune having been spent on period costumes, props and vehicles. But whatever the reason for its termination after just 13 episodes, the short life of the show was a disappointment for Clarke.

First of the Summer Wine.
Left to right: David Fenwick (Clegg), Richard Lumsden (Foggy), and Paul Wyett (Compo)
(Malcolm Howarth)

MAN OF HOLMFIRTH

As the 1980s ended, Holmfirth was well and truly on the map as a tourist destination and a pleasant and desirable place to live. And Bill Owen's place as an honorary citizen of the town was assured. Owen was still in demand for interviews and personal appearances, never wasting an opportunity to boost and promote Holmfirth, and still throwing himself into charity work and good causes of all kinds. Friends of Owen's in the town included the Hinchliffes and the Dunnills, and he also developed a close relationship with photographer Malcolm Howarth.

MALCOLM: 'What sort of man was Bill Owen? Well, he was a Londoner, but you've got to forgive him for that haven't you? Seriously, he was a decent fella, that's for sure. I had a good friendship with Bill and that developed through his involvement with the Air Training Corps which met at the Drill Hall in Holmfirth. He became their president and he asked me to go there one night to photograph him presenting a trophy to a lad of his choosing, something he did every year. Bill pointed a boy out to me and said, "I'm awarding the trophy to that guy this year. He comes every time, never misses. He never does anything remarkable, but he's faithful and reliable, he plods on and gets the job done, doing his best week after week." I totally got where Bill was coming from. It could turn a lad's life around, getting noticed like that. Receiving an

Holmfirth Turn Again Theatre players Rob Dixon, Nigel Hinchliffe, and Jack Dunnill
(Jack Dunnill)

award for his efforts would make him feel appreciated, make him puff his chest out and hold his shoulders back, and feel that he was special and counted for something after all. Bill asked me to go to the Drill Hall quite a few times after that for various ATC things. It was a wooden hut basically. They had a rifle range in

there, but it was more like a tube they fired down!'

JENNY HINCHLIFFE: : 'Bill was quite a serious person, you know, and very into his politics. He was quite left wing, and a Labour supporter through and through. He wasn't from a wealthy background. And he was quite a serious actor. I think he set out to be another James Cagney at one time.'

MALCOLM: 'Bill was most definitely a Labour man. I remember him once giving up a Saturday to speak at a Miners' Gala at Barnsley. In those days there were thousands at these events. Scargill would spout and I'd be there photographing him. On this occasion Bill was invited and he asked me about Barnsley, if there was anywhere decent to eat. He'd got London ways; I imagined him there, tucking his napkin down his collar. I said I didn't know if there would be anywhere up to his standards. But I did notice that day how down to earth he was. He didn't just turn up at the rally and give a speech. He marched through the town with the miners, right at the front of the parade with Scargill and the NUM officials. When it came to politics, he wore his heart on his sleeve.'

JENNY: 'When Bill met people as himself, I think they could sometimes be a bit disappointed he wasn't cracking jokes all the time. But he could be very funny, quite witty, and ironic. We went out with him for a meal once at a slightly well-to-do country restaurant. Bill's meal was a bit dry and he asked for some gravy

Happy to endorse local businesses, Bill Owen poses in costume in front of Compo's Cafe (formerly Parkhead Fisheries), and a now real-life Sid's Café
(Malcolm Howarth)

and the waitress said, "I'm not a slave, you know!" and Bill was dumbfounded. He couldn't think of anything to say to that. No "I'll see what I can do for you" or anything like that. And then no gravy came, so he had to ask her again. I think some people were frightened of feeling they were kowtowing to these supposedly important people, famous actors or whatever. They didn't like the idea of that and would react in funny ways. Rather than being polite, they'd try to assert themselves. "Don't be thinking you're more special than us…" Well, of course he was special, and he did a lot of very good things for Holmfirth. He absolutely loved Holmfirth.'

JACK DUNNILL: 'He loved everything about the place. You could ask him to do anything and he would try to help. Take the amateur dramatic group Turn Again Theatre, which we founded in 1987. Bill became our lifetime honorary president and spoke the first words ever said on stage by anyone in the group. He was a talking tree, and we recorded his lines at our house. Peter Sallis and Brian Wilde were nice enough people, but they had no great interest in the town – not in the same way.'

MALCOLM: 'Before filming began for each series he'd ring me from London and ask me to reserve him a table at a restaurant he liked in Huddersfield called Trattoria Alla Scala. He'd say, "Say it's for me, and tell them I want a Dover sole." It wasn't on the menu, but they'd order one specially for him. Once he arrived in Holmfirth I'd pick him up and take him to the restaurant, and when we sat down he'd ask me to fill him in on all the gossip since his last visit… what Nigel Hinchliffe had been up to, how Dorothy Gregg was getting on at the Wrinkled Stocking Tea Room and what my news was. And when the meal was served the sole would arrive on a hot tray and they'd cut it up at the side of the plate. But the filleting would have to be perfect. On one occasion the waiter wasn't serving it to Bill's satisfaction and he stood up and showed him how to do it. He was a man of the people, no question, but he could be a bit snooty on occasion, especially when it came to his food. Everything had to be right.'

JACK: 'Bill was a smashing man, a lovely man. And because of that, and because of his attitude to the town, we tried to pay him back for his kindness. Beryl did some typing for him, and when he asked me to compere a couple of Bill Owen charity nights at the Civic Hall in Holmfirth, I said yes of course I would, I didn't mind at all. A friend of ours, Dorothy Gregg, was involved with him in setting them up to raise money for local charities. Bill loved doing things like that. They got

Bill Owen on stage at Holmfirth Civic Hall
(Malcolm Howarth)

some very good acts too: Bolsterstone Choir, some excellent local musicians including a couple of top level pianists - Dorothy could get these people - so it was easy enough for me to go on and tell a few jokes and introduce the various acts, which included Bill himself, of course. Bill would do a monologue and sing a song or two. They were sell-outs and very successful.'

MALCOLM: 'Bill was kept busy on his time off. We'd be on set filming and people would sidle up and ask, "Can you get to so-and-so place tonight to have a photograph taken with us?" Not only would he usually say yes, he'd provide me with bits and pieces of work because I'd get paid per picture by the Holme Valley Express, much to the annoyance of the editor and the reporters sometimes because the first they knew about it was when a picture dropped in the editor's in-tray.

Signing for a fan
(Malcolm Howarth)

'He was always particularly keen to help young people. If any youth club asked him to come, he'd put himself out to help. He must have had loads of requests where he thought, "Oh gawd, I really don't want to do that," but he'd always turn up. Anything for Holmfirth, basically. Never charged a penny to my knowledge. The ATC did a gala once a year and Bill got the whole of the Summer Wine cast, without exception, to attend by horse and cart, through the recreation grounds by the river at Sands. He got marquees put up, and arranged for the army to come, and he said I'd like to display some Summer Wine memorabilia and you've got hundreds of pictures. Can you put something together for us? So I made a big display of 20x16 pictures on easels and stands. That was the beginnings of what became the Summer Wine Exhibition, an add-on to my photography business and an enterprise that's still going today.

'I got to know the cast much better through working with Bill on that. It was a lot of work for a temporary display but it became the basis of a permanent exhibition Bill and I set up in Jack and Beryl's former premises on Hollowgate, a building that's now Simon Blyth estate agents. Bill got himself very involved. He had a lot of ideas for the exhibition and he'd say to the props department things like, "This motorbike, what's going on with it when we're done?" In the series it was a heavy motorbike that fell over spewing oil all over Wesley, but it wasn't real oil, and it wasn't a real motorbike either. It wasn't at all heavy. You could lift it up with two fingers! It

was made of polystyrene but absolutely brilliantly done – you couldn't tell. The special effects department had made it, and eventually, years later, they reclaimed it. Bill used his influence to get me things like that, props like the large lady who went floating off into the sky, a submarine, and all kinds of other bits and pieces. He wasn't a business partner; in fact, he didn't take anything at all from the business. He was just my friend and we were partners in putting the exhibition together. He also helped me set up some of my photo sessions and gave me pictures from his own collection.

'When he was staying in Holmfirth I'd drive over from Barnsley every Saturday and take him to Marks and Spencers in Huddersfield to stock up his fridge for the week. Salmon, fish pie - he did eat a lot of fish. Then on the way home we'd stop off at the Jacob's Well pub in Honley which was highly regarded at the time for its roast beef sandwiches. He'd have one of those and a pint of Guinness. Then I'd drop him home and go off and do all my Saturday afternoon photography jobs, football matches and what have you. And on some occasions he'd say he'd got nothing on, and rather than take him back to his bungalow I'd drop him off at the exhibition and he'd sit there signing pictures and books for all the people who came in.

'The exhibition never really made money, truth be told, but it was popular with visitors and useful for bringing people in to buy my photographs. We ordered some mugs with my pictures on and slowly built up a fair stock of

Bill at Malcolm Howarth's Summer Wine Exhibition
(Malcolm Howarth)

interesting souvenirs, such as Compo hats made by a lady in Honley who also supplied them to Bill. One way and another we built the business up. We moved twice, and in the finish I ended up in Bamforths' old studio on the main road out of Holmfirth to New Mill. It was the building where their artists used to draw the saucy postcards. I used that building as my photographic studio for a long while and it would amuse me to imagine the postcard artists gazing out of the first floor window, using the fat ladies of Holmfirth for inspiration!'

Adverts for Malcolm Howarth's Summer Wine exhibition

Motorised mayhem was a regular theme
(Malcolm Howarth)

DOROTHY GREGG

Perhaps more than any other resident, tea-room proprietor Dorothy Gregg was an enthusiastic champion of Holmfirth. She was fundamental to the town's successful reinvention as a tourist destination, and instrumental in it becoming a more desirable place to live.

JACK DUNNILL: 'Dorothy was the guiding light behind so many things and a great help to the Summer Wine team because they all knew her, and she helped them in any way she could. She also worked tirelessly to promote the town, to improve the town, and to encourage tourism. She pioneered tourism in Holmfirth in many ways.'

BERYL DUNNILL: 'Dorothy was a wonderful person and very much undervalued. Her kitchen at the Wrinkled Stocking Tea Room was Compo's bedroom in the series and whenever they were filming outside she'd have to clear it because they could see through the window. But she didn't mind at all. She was friendly and close to everyone on the set and she'd be as cooperative as she could.'

JENNY HINCHLIFFE: 'When she opened the Wrinkled Stocking Tea Room, I designed the tableware for it, the plates and cups and saucers, and the teapots. Oh gosh, they did sell a lot! The Duchess of York came to Holmfirth one day to open something or other and attended a function afterwards at the Old Bridge Hotel. Getting wind of this, Dorothy shot home, got all dressed up in her best outfit, and came back with a tray of Wrinkled Stocking crockery. She held it up as the duchess was setting off after the 'do', and Sarah Ferguson stopped the car, jumped out and ran over to Dot and took a Nora Batty teapot. "Thank you very much," she said, "I'm going to give it to the Queen Mother." There were press photographs taken of this and of course Dot made the most of them.'

MALCOLM: "I got on very well with Dorothy. She was the president of the Holmfirth Chamber of Trade the year before I was. It's the Holme Valley Business Association now. When she was president, Bill Owen bought a seat for the town and they put it in the park. Dorothy organised that. The bungalow where Bill stayed was owned by a talented carpenter called Harry Beaumont. Harry made the bench, which is still in daily use in the entrance hall of Holmfirth Civic Hall."

JACK: 'Every year we'd have a shopping week, a whole week of events, and Dorothy was always very much to the fore. Obviously, she was promoting her own business but she was also promoting Holmfirth.'

MALCOLM: 'She was a tourism pioneer. She was energetic and hard-working and full of ideas, and she'd have done more, only she was suppressed a little by some of her neighbours. She had plans to extend the Wrinkled Stocking and was going to call the new bit the Fancy Ferret. When the BBC heard about it, they helped all they could. She had a wall knocked through and it was going to be a big surprise for Bill. I was set to move my exhibition in next door. But neighbours put paid to the plan. The owner of a knick-knack type shop tucked away up there didn't want more people going up. Very strange.'

JENNY: 'Dorothy made the Wrinkled Stocking into a very successful business. She acted with Turn Again Theatre, was very artistic, and was very good at encouraging people. Her husband, Tommy, would never dream of acting but he was very practical and could make almost anything. They were a very good team.'

BERYL: 'Dorothy got the River Holme cleaned up in the middle of Holmfirth. She got 90 people to donate £90 each in 1990. She got some builders to give her free use of a JCB digger, although we had to pay the driver's wages. Our young grandson sat on the top of it as it trundled along the riverbed.'

Dorothy Gregg with a Jenny Hinchliffe plate
(Jack Dunnill)

The Wrinkled Stocking Tea Room - named in Nora's honour!

Bill's bench. A gift to Holmfirth
(Malcolm Howarth)

JENNY: 'Dot did amazing work cleaning up the river, together with David Earnshaw from Kaye's hardware shop. Many volunteers put in time and effort and I salute them all, but Dot and David were the chief organisers. Dot and I worked well together on a Youth Against Crime drama competition, involving teams of young people from local high schools, the Guides and other organisations. I got Alan Bell to be a judge alongside other prominent TV people, including Roy Clarke. Nobody could believe it when they came. Dot did a super supper for them at the Wrinkled Stocking and then we all went to Holmfirth High School where the kids put on a series of short plays. They were very good and included one where there were little girl guides sniffing cocaine, I recall! The judges cast their votes and Shelley High won. The VIP guests all really enjoyed it. Roy Clarke was charming, and his wife was perfectly pleasant too, but a year or so later when his character Hyacinth Bucket first appeared on our screens, it occurred to me she might have been the inspiration. That's the way these things work sometimes!'

Shopping Week in Holmfirth!
(Malcolm Howarth)

Weather in the Holme Valley
(Howard Allen)

LAST OF THE SUMMER WINE

Please note the following additional points:

1   *Because of the rapidly changing weather in the
     Holmfirth area, it is often necessary to move locations,
     sometimes Location Bases and it has even been known to
     change scenes to be filmed at very short notice.*

2   *Stand-ins for COMPO/CLEGG/FOGGY are on call every day.*

3   *Would all Staff making their own accommodation
     arrangements please give their address and telephone
     number to the Production Assistant, Gail Evans,
     on Day 1.*

4   *This schedule is only an intention, not the definitive
     version.*

ALL GOOD THINGS...

Series 11 of Last Of The Summer Wine was broadcast in October and November 1989 and concluded with a Christmas Special shown on December 23. This would be the last episode of the show with Seymour as a main character. While the series was being filmed, Michael Aldridge had received distressing messages from friends and neighbours. His wife was suffering from dementia and becoming increasingly confused. It became clear he could no longer leave her to go away for work. Seymour Utterthwaite made a final, brief appearance in the first episode of the 1990 series, telling his chums he was leaving Holmfirth to come out of retirement and take up a post as a relief headmaster. Aldridge was 69 at the time and he died aged 73, survived by his wife. Seymour having left, Clegg said, poignantly, "Suddenly life is like first class mail. There doesn't appear to be any urgency anymore."

The same episode that saw Seymour's departure featured the return of Foggy Dewhurst, with Brian Wilde back in the role having been persuaded by Alan Bell. This time he would stay with the series for a run of eight years before hanging up his cap and walking stick for a second time, and retiring, in 1997.

The 1990 series consisted of ten episodes plus a Christmas special, and Clarke's writing was as crisp and funny as ever. It was this series in which Bell introduced the choreographed coffee drinking at Edie's ladies' get-togethers, and the participants' polite yet steely competition for the last chocolate eclair.

The 1990s was a second golden era for the show. For some time now episodes had tended to follow a familiar formula, ending in chaos as everything went wrong. The audience didn't mind an element of predictability. In fact they loved it, revelling in anticipation and enjoying an eventual reward. The Pennine countryside continued to delight, and viewers were seeing more of it than ever, with Alan Bell shooting more and more in Yorkshire, and less and less in the studio, until, in 1992, he began filming each episode entirely on location. Bill Owen and some of the other theatre-oriented members of the cast missed the studio sessions. They enjoyed the feel and atmosphere of being on a stage set, and the sound of real laughter during their performances. That is not to say the chuckles and belly laughs on the soundtracks in those years are not genuine; complete episodes were shown to audiences in preview screenings, where their laughter was recorded and stars from the show entertained them before the event. With each new series, Roy Clarke continued to turn out episodes on demand and to a consistently high standard. His output

The old gang back together again!
Foggy Dewhurst returned to the series when Seymour was called away.
(Malcolm Howarth)

during this period is remarkable considering the volume of other work he produced at the same time. The filmic nature of the show, and with so much exterior action, was tough on an ageing cast: madcap escapades needed space, Howard and Marina's adventures were always outdoors, and the ladies were forever at large in that death-trap of a car. Bell made more use of stand-ins but there was still a lot of walking, cycling, and standing around.

RIGHT: Old school!
(Malcolm Howarth)

Synchronised sipping
(Malcolm Howarth)

Howard and Marina are foiled again as another plan goes terribly wrong!
(Malcolm Howarth)

In his element. Portrait of a happy man
(Malcolm Howarth)

Owen was 80 in 1994; still promoting Holmfirth, still enjoying stardom, still fired by politics, still doing charity work, and still acting superbly well and being paid handsomely for his efforts.

Despite his age he remained elegant and graceful in his movement, and as an actor he remained deft, superb at clowning, and an expert judge of timing.

And although Compo's characterisation had come to him in an almost fully-realised form, Owen continued to draw on sources around him to tweak and perfect his creation.

MALCOLM: 'As an actor he'd be listening and looking all the time. He might even have picked some little things up from me. He did mimic me sometimes. He observed people in Holmfirth; how they walked and talked, their mannerisms. How they wouldn't be polite – a Holmfirth trait. Quite often on a morning Bill would walk down Dunford Road from his house at Underbank into Holmfirth and get picked up by one of the drivers. He'd call in at Nigel Hinchliffe's for a paper and a chat. Other customers would come in, and they'd stand and talk. Outside, people would call out and he'd wave his paper. All the while he'd be listening and looking. He'd pick up on it all.'

Owen was old school, but a bit of a method actor too, assuming Compo's persona easily when in costume and happy to spend time as his alter ego, fooling with kids on location between set-ups. Clegg remained the philosopher of the trio. Like Peter Sallis who played him, he was intelligent, astute, witty, and dry. Clegg was also a little unworldly. Terrified of going near Auntie Wainwright's shop, he was also mortally afraid of Pearl, and getting trapped in a lift with Marina once frightened him a great deal!

Brian Wilde was more mellow second time around, easier company and less awkward to deal with. He had been given a second chance on a major series after a few lean years, and for this he was grateful; although he continued to stay at the Hilton near the M62 and did not generally socialise with the rest of the cast.

MALCOLM: 'He stayed at Ainley Top, about half an hour's drive away. He wasn't a good mixer, Brian, and he and Bill were never close, but they got along well enough second time around.'

Foggy continued to be authoritarian, a man of action, a restless bundle of energy and a hatcher of hare-brained schemes. He continued to regale all and sundry with improbable, if not totally absurd tales of jungle derring-do. Yes, Foggy was completely bonkers, but Wilde underplayed the part to the point of genius, making him an impeccably realised as well as exquisitely drawn sitcom character.

Foggy Dewhurst has gone down in history as the nation's favourite Summer Wine third man, which is not to underestimate in any way the unique talents of Michael Bates and Michael Aldridge; or indeed Frank Thornton or any of the other very fine comedy actors who followed on from Wilde in the series' later years. Meanwhile, Nora Batty remained a woman too dreadful to be attractive in so many ways. Bossy, a gossip, and a scold, and forever in wrinkled stockings, yet Compo, scuttling out from his underdwelling as keenly as ever, remained besotted. It is to Bill Owen's great credit that Compo's lusting and leering was never in bad taste, and to Kathy Staff's that Nora always maintained her dignity.

While there was still time for the old men to mooch and meander, the number of strong supporting actors in the expanded cast allowed for simultaneous storylines and an overall increase in pace. And the supporting actors were becoming firm fan favourites in their own right. Matriarchal Edie, tinkering Wesley and gentle Glenda; brusque Ivy and acidic Pearl; furtive Howard and lovelorn Marina; the misnamed Smiler and stingy Auntie Wainwright; myopic Eli and cowardly policemen (various), all had their following.

The programme became reliable Sunday evening entertainment and audiences still hovered around the ten million mark. Good for the times considering the recent advent of satellite broadcasting and video recorders having become commonplace.

In 1996 it was revealed Last Of The Summer Wine was the Queen's favourite television programme. That same year Mike Grady returned to the show, having been absent for six years working on other projects. But as his character was frequently mentioned during his absence, Barry slotted straight back in. Grady and

Off-duty Bill Owen attending a function (the stubble denotes the picture was taken during filming)
(Malcolm Howarth)

Man of the jungle!
(Malcolm Howarth)

Sarah Thomas worked exceptionally well together and shared an ability to learn lines extremely quickly. On a few occasions an episode would be found to be running short, and an additional scene would be requested from Clarke to make up running time. He'd usually write something self-contained for Glenda and Barry, and Thomas and Grady would deliver a perfect performance at short notice.

Intelligent and astute, Peter Sallis as Norman Clegg
(Malcolm Howarth)

Compo embraces Nora, but she is not impressed!
(Malcolm Howarth)

CATERING: Rolls available from 0830.
                         Lunch 1245.
                         Tea and coffee TBA.

SPECIAL REQS
AND PROPS: Moby crane
                         Mat and beater
                         Nora's broom
                         Smiler's suitcases

TO SHOOT: 1) Ep 8 (Sc 1) EXT NORA'S
                             (2.25 pgs)
                             COMPO/NORA
                             Compo creeps up on Nora
                             whilst she's beating a
                             mat.

                         2) Ep 8 (Sc 7) EXT NORA'S
                             (3.5 pgs)
                             COMPO/CLEGG/FOGGY/NORA
                             Compo embraces Nora but
                             she is not impressed.

                         3) Ep 8 (Sc 18) EXT COMPO'S
                             (2 pgs)
                             COMPO/CLEGG/FOGGY/NORA
                             They watch as Nora comes
                             towards Compo's door.

                         4) Ep 10 (Sc 25) EXT NORA'S
                             (0.5 pg)
                             COMPO/CLEGG/FOGGY/NORA/
                             SMILER
                             Smiler enters Nora's
                             with his suitcases.

                         5) Ep 10 (Sc 1) EXT NORA'S
                             (2.5 pgs)
                             COMPO/NORA
                             Compo asks Nora to elope.

EST WRAP: 1715

A stag's head and a cast iron bathtub? Don't ask!
(Malcolm Howarth)

Barry and Glenda... and Compo

(Malcolm Howarth)

Guest Stars

Matthew Kelly and Jean Alexander
(Malcolm Howarth)

Keith Marsh
(Malcolm Howarth)

Peter Sallis, Ron Moody, Brian Wilde and Bill Owen
(Malcolm Howarth)

Bill Owen and Gordon Kaye
(Malcolm Howarth)

Malcolm Hebden
(Malcolm Howarth)

Jean Rogers
(Malcolm Howarth)

Kris Akabusi
(Malcolm Howarth)

Guest stars were queueing up to appear in the show. Cardew (the Cad) Robinson played another henpecked husband, and John Cleese appeared in a sci-fi Christmas special. Malcolm Hebden (Coronation Street), Jean Rogers (Dolly in Emmerdale), and Gordon Kaye (famous as Rene in Allo Allo) also all appeared. So did the athlete Kriss Akabusi, the Stars In Their Eyes and Game For A Laugh presenter Matthew Kelly, and Ron Moody, the definitive Fagin. Another big name, Norman Wisdom, starred in a New Year's Day special in 1995 entitled The Man Who Nearly Knew Pavarotti, and made five more appearances after that.

NORMAN WISDOM

Norman Wisdom was a massively famous comedy film star from the 1950s and 1960s and a brilliant visual comic. He was a championship-winning flyweight boxer in the army during the Second World War, and from his boxing moves he began to develop his distinctive comedic routines involving pratfalls and gormless facial expressions. He was also a talented dancer and musician, but he did not become a professional entertainer until he was aged 31, a year after being demobbed.

When three became four. The Summer Wine trio together with the irrepressible Norman Wisdom
(Malcolm Howarth)

Time to go!
(Malcolm Howarth)

Wisdom first joined the cast of Summer Wine aged 79 but still bursting with energy. He was a terrible scene stealer and rather full of himself, but his body acting was still extraordinary and his timing as sharp as ever. Fabulously fit, he behaved like a man half his age, sliding, falling, and pirouetting in mesmeric fashion. Altogether, he was a terrific entertainer, although his motormouth tendency reportedly got on Peter Sallis's nerves from time to time. In The Man Who Nearly Knew Pavarotti, Wisdom's character, Billy Ingleton, was a mad-keen but ultimately useless musician, desperate to give a piano recital.

MALCOLM: 'Norman Wisdom! What can I say about that guy? He was fantastic. Just a complete idiot. A big personality and an absolutely lovely fella. He was very well liked by everyone. A nice guy. We were filming at Marsden Mechanics Institute for The Man Who Nearly Knew Pavarotti. The gag was Billy Ingleton could play a spectacular intro to a piece of piano music absolutely brilliantly, note perfect, but that's all he knew, he couldn't play the piece itself. He did his scene, playing the intro superbly and collapsing and falling off his stool at the end of it because Billy fainted when he couldn't carry on. But the real Norman Wisdom definitely could have carried on, I'm sure of that, because he was a gifted musician and he could play most instruments. When we were done with filming that day some of the crew were in a side room and he came in and started entertaining us, telling jokes, laughing, messing about. Then he played the clarinet for us, absolutely beautifully. Anyone else you'd think he was showing off, but he wasn't, it was just him. It wasn't a case of, "I'm Norman Wisdom, I'm famous, you get out of my way." None of that. He'd go into character in the middle of a conversation and perform to you in private. You wouldn't need to ask him.

'He'd also have a joke with the crew. I remember shooting another scene with him in Marsden. There was quite a long chat between his character, Billy Ingleton, and two other main characters. A long track was laid so the camera could run alongside them as they talked together walking down a long lane. At the end of the dialogue, the camera swung round and the other two stopped, leaving Billy carrying on a bit on his own. That was the end of the shot. By then they'd be quite a way from us all, probably fifty yards, and the assistant director shouted, "Cut!" "Fine for me, thanks," said Alan Bell. "Norman, we've cut!" shouted the AD [assistant director], but on and on Norman went, up and over the hill at the end of the lane and completely out of sight down the other side. We all looked at one another, then everybody in the crew started laughing. Eventually Norman peeked back over the hill. He waved his cap, and shouted at the top of his voice, "Was that okay?" Then he stuck his chest out, put his cap on the back of his head, and went into classic Norman Wisdom mode. He did his funny rolling walk for a few moments, then he jogged briskly all the way back. Remarkable really - it was a long way but he was a very fit guy for his age. And when he got back to us he tapped Doug, one of the camera crew guys, on the shoulder and said, "Come on, I'll race you back up to the top of the hill".'

TRULY INSPIRED

As filming on series 19 drew near, Brian Wilde was approaching 70 and feeling his years. He asked Alan Bell if he and Roy Clarke wouldn't mind downgrading his character, giving him a less exacting schedule with fewer days on location. But then Wilde fell ill with shingles and although he eventually made a full recovery, and Bell and others made overtures, he never returned to the show, feeling that after 116 episodes, enough was enough. What to do? Alan Bell invited experienced sitcom actor Frank

Preparing to shoot a scene for There Goes The Groom
(Malcolm Howarth)

Thornton to lunch along with Thora Hird, Jean Alexander and Stephen Lewis; and to the 76-year-old veteran performer's surprise and delight, invited him to take over the third man role. The actor had presumed he was being sized up for a guest appearance. Clarke got busy with rewrites and Thornton took part in six episodes in series 19, plus a Christmas special, There Goes the Groom, which dealt with Foggy's departure, and in which unit photographer Malcolm Howarth made a key cameo performance.

Another strong line-up
(Malcolm Howarth)

PETER SALLIS

FRANK THORNTON

BILL OWEN

Truly ends up drenched and Howard and Marina's fishy plans are foiled!

(Malcolm Howarth)

MALCOLM: 'It was one of a number occasions over the years when Alan Bell said, "Here Malc, we need you to pretend to be a photographer!" I said, "No problem, I've been doing that for years!" On this occasion I had to play a wedding photographer who, in the last scene of the episode, takes a phone call from Foggy saying he's been kidnapped and gone to live in Blackpool. I pass on the news and that event marks the end of the second Foggy era and confirms Truly as the new third man.'

Having previously been used mostly as a supporting character throughout his long career, or as part of an ensemble cast, Thornton took a little while to adjust his deferential acting style to suit a leading role. But with Peter Sallis being especially supportive, he soon adapted. Thornton praised Clarke's sophisticated writing as an aid in this, adding that because his lines rang so true, learning them was never a chore. Frank Thornton was perhaps best known by the British public as ex-military man Captain Peacock, the stern and snooty floorwalker in Are You Being Served?, the BBC department store-based sitcom. This much-loved classic series ran from 1972 to 1985,

plus a spin-off called Grace and Favour in 1992. Because of this association, Thornton was another familiar friend of the show's core audience, exactly like Bell's conspiratorial luncheon guests Jean Alexander, Thora Hird and Stephen Lewis.

Thornton was a tall, upright man with a sombre but highly expressive face. An RAF flying officer in the Second World War, like Sallis he was a member of the Garrick Club, and the two had worked together on stage. In 1961 he appeared with Tony Hancock in perhaps that comedian's most famous television episode, The Blood Donor, written by Galton and Simpson. He subsequently made guest appearances in several Steptoe and Son series by the same writers.

Thornton also worked with Benny Hill, Michael Bentine, Spike Milligan, and Frankie Howerd among many other big names from British television history. As a result, he was popular with the public and highly respected in the profession as a superb comedy actor with pinpoint timing. He was a modest man who fitted in well with the Summer Wine cast and crew. His character was retired policeman Herbert Truelove, the self-

proclaimed Truly Of The Yard; a pompous and authoritative individual who still very much liked to be in command. There were echoes of Blamire in that he was always smartly turned out in raincoat, police tie and trilby hat, and he was reminiscent of Foggy when he launched into improbable tales about his past crime-fighting exploits.

He spoke gravely about a dreadful, unseen ex-wife, recalling a long and dreary marriage. But despite the aforementioned traits, Truly took himself a little less seriously than his third man predecessors, and he was generally more liked and respected by the other characters in the show.

MALCOLM: 'Frank Thornton was a decent guy. A normal fella doing a job. Highly professional, straight up and down, no messing anybody about, and everyone got on with him just fine.'

Thornton's gloomy Truly remained a key character in Last Of The Summer Wine until its final series in 2010, and Peter Sallis, too, would outlive the programme, but as the 20th century neared its end, the show's biggest star was unknowingly approaching his final act.

On a Holme Valley hilltop
(Malcolm Howarth)

Visiting Auntie Wainwright's. Clegg clearly needs some persuasion
(Malcolm Howarth)

Late century action
(Malcolm Howarth)

Working in a controlled environment
(Malcolm Howarth)

Over the years many interior scenes were recorded at various London studios
(Malcolm Howarth)

Compo in trouble again!
(Malcolm Howarth)

All is not what it seems.
The BBC Special Effects Department
did the show proud over many years.
(Malcolm Howarth)

Hair and make-up
(Malcolm Howarth)

Town and Country

On location in the Holme Valley
(Malcolm Howarth)

Chapter Eight

BYE BYE BILL

s the 1990s drew to a close, Compo was as irrepressibly roguish as ever, retaining his chirpy, childlike quality and knock-about physicality. When the camera rolled, Bill Owen threw off the years, springing around like a man less than half his age. And off set he was easy-going and content, less prickly and sensitive. Kathy Staff had taken to looking after him, telling Alan Bell if she thought he was demanding too much.

Roy Clarke wrote a special to be broadcast on January 2, 2000, taking the show that had started as a one-off at the beginning of the 1970s, confidently into the new millennium. The episode involved a new backstory element for Compo, taking him back sixty years to the Dunkirk evacuation of 1940. The episode would require serious acting from Owen as well as his comedic talents. Shooting took the trio to France and there were scenes on a ferry on the way.

But as soon as filming started it was clear Owen was unwell. He lacked energy, seemed disconnected and struggled badly with his lines. But he soldiered on. Then the cast and crew travelled to Holmfirth, by which time Owen was visibly tired and clearly very ill indeed. He had pancreatic cancer, a late diagnosis, and while on set he was given just six to eight weeks to live, although it's possible he did not know the full facts straight away; it was his doctor who told Alan Bell the grim prognosis, not Owen himself. But he certainly knew

All's fair in love and war! Bill Owen's knock-about physicality endured until the end
(Malcolm Howarth)

Saying goodbyes
(Malcolm Howarth)

Scenes from Bill Owen's favourite episode: From Wellies To Wetsuit, first shown in 1982
(Don Smith)

he was very ill indeed, and in different ways he was saying his goodbyes.

MALCOLM HOWARTH: 'The cast and crew went to France and filmed quite a bit over there, and then they came back up here to film what were Bill's last ever scenes. It wasn't nice. I could see him suffering and I couldn't step onto the set to prop him up because when you're on a film set everyone's got their job, and there were people there whose responsibility it was to deal with him. There were times I was longing to walk in and help. I could see him bending down sometimes, doubling up in pain. He really suffered. He was beginning to lose the firmness in his face. His skin was hanging off him. It was a sorry sight, and it was upsetting. When we'd done filming for the day, it was other people's responsibility then to take him home and fetch him again in the morning, but I would have done it, gladly. I really wanted to do it as a friend, but it wasn't my place. I did take him shopping on his days off, which was something at least. During this time, they used a location in the countryside near Hepworth, which was supposed to be somewhere in France. There was a pond there and the special effects people set up a little waterfall at the back of it. The three men were supposed to be travelling through France on a motorcycle and sidecar and they'd pulled off somewhere where a

Summit conference. On A Holme Valley hilltop.
(Malcolm Howarth)

friend of Compo's had died in the war. They set some doves off, or pigeons, and Compo played The Last Post on a bugle for his army mate. Oh dear, it was incredibly moving. There wasn't a dry eye anywhere in the crew as Bill put the bugle to his lips because everybody knew Bill was dying as well.

'Everybody on set knew what was happening but it was a strange time. He was poorly the whole time he was filming that last series and I'm sure he knew he was dying. He said to Peter Sallis at one point he didn't want to die, that he'd far too much to do. I was there. Peter had no words and was clearly fighting back a tear or two. Somehow or other, Bill finished his filming commitments in Yorkshire and then there was the studio stuff to do.'

Owen completely exhausted himself finishing enough scenes for three episodes of series 21 on location and also in the studio in London. Then he went home and suffered a stroke, dying in the King Edward VII Hospital soon afterwards. The date of his death was July 12, 1999. He was 85 years old. Peter Sallis visited him on the day he died, and so did his son Tom, who was working as a drama teacher in the capital. The following day the BBC transmitted Owen's favourite Summer Wine episode, From Wellies To Wet Suit, directed by Alan Bell and first shown in 1982. Some years before, the Yorkshire Society had made Owen an honorary Yorkshireman, and in his will, he made a specific request to be buried in the graveyard of St. John's Church, in Upperthong, overlooking Holmfirth. He'd also told Peter Sallis this wish several years earlier.

MALCOLM: 'Bill once told me he and Peter had been sitting high on a Holme Valley hillside together looking down

across the meadows to St John's with Holmfirth beyond, and Bill had said: "This is where I want to be buried, Peter, looking down over Holmfirth." And that's exactly what he got.'

A quiet funeral was held, with Peter Sallis and Roy Clarke in attendance. Sallis, whose character Clegg was closer to Compo than the various third men, was visibly upset. Later, there was a memorial service in Holmfirth Parish Church and another organised by the BBC in London.

MALCOLM: 'Bill's funeral was a family only affair, but quite a few locals who'd got to know him went along and stood outside to show their respect. I think I was the only one of the crew to join them. Peter Sallis attended the funeral, and Bill's son Tom Owen, whom I later got to know very well. Peter is buried there now, in the same place.'

Compo's last resting place. Bill Owen's grave,
St. John's Church, Upperthong, Holmfirth
(Howard Allen)

Here Lies
Wm. J. Owen Rowbotham
Actor / Playwright
14. 03. 1914 – 12. 07. 1999

R.I.P.

Dedicated
by his
wife Kathie   "n.m.n"

Visibly moved. Truly and Clegg at Compo's funeral
(Malcolm Howarth)

Liz Fraser was Compo's secret girlfriend, Regina, and got to inherit his ferrets
(Malcolm Howarth)

Barry and friend
(Malcolm Howarth)

Last respects. Setting up a scene for Compo's funeral
(Malcolm Howarth)

Looking forward
(Malcolm Howarth)

A regretful Nora approves of Tom
(Malcolm Howarth)

Bill Owen's son Tom came into the series as Compo's son, also Tom. The dog was called Waldo
(Malcolm Howarth)

Mrs Avery (Julie T Wallace) and her niece, Babs (Helen Turner), make their debuts
(Malcolm Howarth)

THE SHOW MUST GO ON

Series 21 had to be completed. Five episodes out of eleven had been shot or recorded, with the other six at various stages of preparation.

MALCOLM: 'After Bill died, Roy Clarke had to amend the episodes he had appeared in and write new ones to explain Compo's death. He had to write Bill out, basically. It was a lot of work which he did in a very short time, and he did a fantastic job of it. It was all very sad, but Bill had died in the middle of a series and there was a great deal of money tied up. It had to be done and Bill wouldn't have had it any other way.'

Clarke came up with a trilogy of episodes that covered the death of Compo, and then four more to move the story on. It was brilliant writing, managing to be funny despite the delicate and desperately sad subject matter. No doubt fired by emotion and adrenalin, Compo's death episodes were written by Clarke in just a few days and Alan Bell did a fine job of completing them on location and in the editing suite. Bell later said, "For a while, under pressure, you do good stuff, but it's only for a while." For a couple of years after Bill Owen's death, there was a sense among the cast and crew that he was with them on location. When filming recommenced after his funeral in 1999, that feeling was especially strong, and Peter Sallis found recording the remainder of series 21 upsetting from time to time. Kathy Staff was also moved, not least because Clarke's new scripts allowed Nora some untypically tender moments. In the rewritten episode which dealt with Compo's death, Nora Batty surprised her long-time admirer dressed in a flapper dress and black stockings. This prompted a massive heart attack from which even the kiss of

Truly and Clegg are not so sure about Tom's baggage
(Malcolm Howarth)

A chip off the old block. Tom Owen doing charitable work at Compo's Cafe, by now a far more substantial establishment
(Malcolm Howarth)

life from the object of his decades-long desires could not save him. At the end of the programme an army of extras was used to spell out, 'See ya Compo' on a Holme Valley hillside. For a couple of years now high definition video had made the Pennine countryside look all the more stunning. Now it helped make the panoramic backdrop particularly poignant. In the following episode, Surprise At Throstlenest, a new character called Regina was revealed to have been Compo's secret girlfriend. Regina was played by Liz Fraser, a nice touch in that the London actress was a friend of Owen's from his days on Carry On films. Fraser, who also appeared as Regina as the story continued in Just A Small Funeral, had been a prolific film comedy actress in the 1960s, and later had an extensive television career.

MALCOLM: 'Liz Fraser had been quite a sex symbol in her time, and she was still a very attractive woman. But she was surprisingly low-key considering she was such a well-known actress. I went in expecting to get a bit of attitude from her, but there was nothing of the sort. Sometimes when you're ordering a well-known person about with a camera in your hand, they don't like it, but she was very pleasant and helpful with a sweet and gentle nature.'

The final four episodes of series 21 brought in Bill Owen's son, Tom, playing Compo's long-lost son, also called Tom. He arrived with a partner, Mrs Avery, and her niece, Babs, who were hippies of sorts.

Howard Sibshaw, conceivably West Yorkshire's most furtive man
(Malcolm Howarth)

Tom Simmonite was intended as a replacement for Compo, but the idea was abandoned, and the character became part of the ensemble cast instead, while the womenfolk in his life were dropped. Tom Simmonite was something of a layabout like his dad, although none too bright. Tom Owen began his career as an assistant stage manager, before taking on acting roles, including for the RSC. In the late 1960s and early 1970s he featured in the all-action, children's

BANG! Wesley emerges from his shed, smoke pellet in his hat!
(Malcolm Howarth)

drama series, Freewheelers, made by Southern Television for ITV. Other significant television work followed and he made a cameo appearance in Last Of The Summer Wine in 1991.

MALCOLM: 'When Tom came in his character was supposed to be some kind of theatrical agent with a talentless female prodigy in tow, but unfortunately for him that storyline didn't work too well and consequently the girl was dropped and he was sidelined a bit. In his father's shadow? Not at all. He's got what it takes to be successful in his own right. He speaks well - I recognise his voice now doing television voice-overs - and he's had various business ventures - acting classes, putting on plays. When he joined the production I thought he was a lovely fella and I got on very well with him. He came over to Barnsley and did a charity quiz for me in my local pub - just the sort of thing his dad would have done. I thought he was a chip off the old block.'

A middle-aged man of 50, Tom Owen joined a soon-to-be expanded cast of veterans of considerably more advanced years, many of them familiar screen favourites and fondly thought of by the British public. Clarke's writing for the series remained bright and individualistic, but inevitably it had become different. His tried and trusted formula which had kept his three leading men at the heart of each script was altered, with the limelight more evenly shared between Clegg and Truly, and his other brilliant older characters, Wesley, Ivy, Nora, Pearl, Howard and Marina, and the devious Auntie Wainwright (who had pretended to be blind to avoid putting money in the collection at Compo's funeral!). Additionally, yet more much-loved veteran British comedy actors would be brought in, some to make one-off appearances, others to turn up on an occasional basis, and a few to become cast regulars.

INTO THE NEW MILLENNIUM

Among the fresh and sometimes hugely familiar faces joining the Summer Wine roster were a number of stand-ins for the role of third man. These included Keith Clifford (Billy Hardcastle), Brian Murphy (Alvin Smedley), and Burt Kwouk (Entwistle). Bert Kwouk joined the series in 2002 as Entwistle from the East, i.e., Hull. An electrician, seller of second-hand washing machines and purveyor of eternal truths, Entwistle was a dry observer in something of a Clegg-like style, and his red Toyota pick-up truck took the place of Wesley's Land Rover as he drove the other men around on their adventures. Born in Lancaster but brought up in Shanghai, Kwouk was a veteran of numerous well-known 1960s British films and television series, and

Entwistle from the East (Burt Kwouk)
(Terry Bartram)

Billy Hardcastle was played over several years by Halifax actor Keith Clifford. White Horse pub landlord Ron Backhouse is the man in the pink shirt
(Malcolm Howarth)

The multiple award-winning Dame Thora Hird continued until 2003 as Edie, here with sister Ros (Dora Bryan), and daughter Glenda (Sarah Thomas)
(Malcolm Howarth)

KATHY STAFF
Nora

BRIAN MURPHY
Alvin

Last of the Summer Wine © BBC

Nora Batty was not Alvin Smedley's biggest fan. Sitcom star Brian Murphy played Alvin
(BBC Publicity Dept)

Danny O'Dea died within a few weeks of Dame Thora Hird in 2003

(Malcolm Howarth)

Fans' favourite, Danny O'Dea
(Malcolm Howarth)

Edie and Seymour's sister, Glenda's Auntie Ros, joined the Summer Wine gang in 2000
(Malcolm Howarth)

famous to a degree for playing Cato Fong, the manic manservant of Peter Sellers' French police inspector Jacques Clouseau, whom he repeatedly ambushed in the Pink Panther films of the 1960s and 1970s. Kwouk was also known for his portrayal of a Japanese army major in the 1980s television series Tenko.

Billy Hardcastle, played by Halifax-born actor Keith Clifford, was a naive character who believed he was a direct descendant of Robin Hood and tried to recruit a band of merry men. Billy moved in next door to Truly and formed a trio for a while with his new neighbour and Norman Clegg.

The character Alvin Smedley was played by another much-loved British comedy actor. Brian Murphy joined the show in the final episode of the 2003 series, playing the new owner and occupant of Compo's underdwelling. Cheeky and cheery, Alvin regularly teased Nora, saying she was in love with him; a preposterous slander which irritated her no end. Murphy, who was born on the Isle of Wight in 1932, met Richard Briers on National Service in the RAF and the two became kindred spirits, determined to pursue acting careers. Back in civvy street, Murphy spent time with Joan Littlewood's Theatre Workshop and as a jobbing actor before finding

Keeping the streets safe in Summer Wine Land over many years were policemen Ken Kitson and Louis Emerick (pictured here), and Ken Capstick
(Malcolm Howarth)

Kathy Staff and Jane Freeman, best of friends
(Malcolm Howarth)

fame in the ITV sitcoms Man About The House (1973-76) and George and Mildred (1976-79). In these he starred as put-upon husband George Roper alongside his long-time friend Yootha Joyce, who played his snobbish wife, Mildred. Although accomplished in many other parts before and since, so masterly were his performances alongside Joyce in these popular programmes that these sitcom roles would largely define him in the public's mind.

Incidentally, Murphy's first episode was Thora Hird's last. Her screen husband Gordon Wharmby had died of cancer in 2002, at which point Hird was 91 and still on good form, having recently won her second and third Best Actress BAFTAs for Alan Bennett's Talking Heads monologue Waiting For The Telegram, and Deric Longden's Lost For Words, directed by Alan Bell. But suddenly she was tiring and her formidable powers were beginning to ebb. Others in the cast stepped up to look after her, not least Jean Alexander, but she fell ill and was hospitalised during the filming of series 24 during 2002. Determined to finish her episodes, Hird left hospital to shoot her interior scenes at Pinewood Studios late that year. She was very frail and needed support, but her performance was as excellent as ever. Dame Thora Hird died in March 2003 and her last episode was

broadcast the following day. Following her death there were references in the show about Edie having died, and in the last three series a framed photo of the character was visible on Barry and Glenda's mantelpiece. Just a few weeks after her death, Danny O'Dea died, aged 92. His final appearance as bumbling, accident-prone Eli had been during 2002.

MALCOLM: 'Danny O'Dea was like Norman Wisdom in that you'd be talking to him and he'd suddenly go into character and do part of his act. I liked Danny. He would do anything for me, that fella. Latterly he was getting very old and losing his memory a little bit, but he'd always help me out in any way he could. He came and switched the Christmas lights on in Holmfirth the year I was president of the Holmfirth Chamber of Trade. When the day came, I helped put the lights up, then I went to Bradford to pick Danny and his wife up from their home. I brought them back to Holmfirth and left them with Dorothy in the Wrinkled Stocking Tea Room while I shot off to get changed and grab the chain of office. I was being as quick as I could but before I could get back to Dorothy's, the town crier, a chap called Malcolm Bates, who was a bit of a character and rather full of himself, decided it was time to head off and start the procession to

the church square ready for the switch-on. So when I got back there were kids in fancy dress coming down the street, fairies flitting about, the Shopping Queen on her throne, people in pantomime costume giving flyers out and goodness knows what else. And walking in front of them all was old Oyez, Oyez! in the cape and hat Dorothy and I had gone to great pains to sort out for him! I thought, they can't start this without me, I've organised it all. And where's Danny? I found him in the Wrinkled Stocking. "I wasn't setting off until you were here," he said. "That town crier was pushy and I knew you'd be here before long." It was the only time I ever saw Danny riled about anything. "I'm not following on at the end," he said. "Tell them all to come back. We're going again with you and me walking at the front." So we did and everything worked out just fine in the end.'

Dora Bryan joined the show in 2000 as Edie and Seymour's long-estranged sister, Ros Utterthwaite. Glenda's Aunt Ros, who was eventually welcomed back into the bosom of the family, often referred to her past relationships, much to Edie's chagrin. Later she became a somewhat unlikely good friend of Pearl Sibshaw. A highly regarded and versatile actress, Bryan had a long and varied career from the 1940s onwards, incorporating both comedic and serious parts, and musical

Latter-day Summer Wine stars on location
(Terry Bartram)

Barry Wilkinson, Man of Action
(Malcolm Howarth)

Nora and Ivy. Formidable women of Holmfirth!
(Malcolm Howarth)

Seymour takes the series forward
(Malcolm Howarth)

An early appearance by
Gordon Wharmby as Wesley
(Malcom Howarth)

Dame Thora Hird as Edie Pegden
(Malcolm Howarth)

Hird was suggested for the role by Bell's wife, Constance. Born in Morecambe in 1911, Hird was the daughter of a theatre manager and first appeared on stage as a babe in arms. It was the start of a career that continued uninterrupted for 92 years. Whether on radio, television, stage, or silver screen, Hird was a star player of character parts. She was down-to-earth, a 'one of us' type of actress who always remembered where she'd come from and had a natural rapport with the general public. She was a household name for most of her life.

Before turning professional she worked as a Co-op shop assistant, then went into rep while still in her teens. After acting in the West End in 1940 she was soon in demand for films while continuing to star on the stage in both plays and variety shows, including at the London Palladium. Television sitcom appearances in the 1960s and 1970s brought her to a new generation of admirers, and one of these programmes, ITV's In Loving Memory, took her to Yorkshire, a county she found she liked very much indeed. Hird could do gritty

drama too and three BAFTA Best Actress awards lay ahead, one for her role in Lost For Words, directed by Alan Bell in 1999. She was also much loved for presenting the Sunday evening religious programme Praise Be! and radio comedy and chat show appearances filled any gaps in her busy schedule.

Dame Thora Hird was aged 74 in 1985 when she joined the cast of Summer Wine for her first guest appearance. Quickly invited back, she became a regular and would ultimately stay with the programme for 17 years.

Her character Edie was different to the other women in the series. She was matriarchal, house-proud and a snob, and inordinately proud of her brother Seymour, who had been 'educated'. In company she would affect a posh, cultured voice which would disappear when she was shouting at her husband, Wesley – 'Wes-lay!' Was Edie a prototype for Hyacinth Bucket? She was certainly concerned about appearances. But like Thora, Edie had a good heart. As Edie became established, so did various behavioural rituals and popular

scenarios. She would bump the house door closed with her backside; Wesley would have to walk on newspapers laid in his path; she became the hostess of innumerable women's coffee mornings; and she would frequently take to the roads around Holmfirth in a red Triumph Herald convertible rebuilt for her by her husband.

Edie was a terrible driver and the passengers in the car, usually the ladies of the coffee morning group, would ride along terror-struck, fearing for their lives. In reality, the cast were more frightened by the car itself. With incurably wayward steering and defective brakes, and doors that flew open unaided or wouldn't open at all, it seemingly had a mind of its own.

If Wesley really had rebuilt the Triumph Herald, it might have been a safer vehicle. For although he drove a battered old Land-Rover and worked in a corrugated tin garage where he tinkered and bodged all manner of madcap mechanical devices, Wesley was basically a competent mechanic, something which rather irked his less than technically proficient brother-in-law, Seymour.

comedy. Her stage successes included winning a Laurence Olivier award in 1995 for her role in Harold Pinter's The Birthday Party at the National Theatre. She appeared in numerous high-profile films over many years, including the first ever Carry On film, Carry On Sergeant, and the unremittingly bleak A Taste of Honey, for which she won the 1962 BAFTA Best Actress Award. She was also a regular performer in radio and television productions.

MALCOLM: 'Like Liz Fraser, Dora Bryan was another big name from British films of the 1960s. She used to talk rather a lot sometimes and was a very nice person, but she wouldn't suffer fools. We had a reporter on set once, another interview I'd arranged, but it didn't go as well as the one I fixed up with Jean Alexander. We sat in Dora's caravan and it soon became clear the reporter had absolutely no idea who Dora was. She hadn't done her homework. In fairness, maybe she'd been thrown in the deep end, but her opening question – "So, have you been in any famous films then?" – didn't go down well, as you can imagine, and there was a frosty atmosphere from then on. But Dora was always as nice as pie with me, and as straight as a die. I knew exactly who she was and that I was respectful of her achievements.'

Cowardly policeman Tony Capstick also died in 2003. He was just 59 years old. The cowardly policemen – PCs Cooper and Walsh – were originally played by Ken Kitson and Louis Emerick respectively, the latter replaced by Capstick. Emerick returned to the show after Capstick's death. Capstick was a comedian and folk singer and bit-part television actor whose credits included a small role in Coronation Street. He was well-known in South Yorkshire as a presenter on BBC Radio Sheffield and as a columnist in the Rotherham Advertiser.

Kitson, from Bradford, first appeared in the show as PC Cooper in Getting Sam Home. Further appearances followed on an occasional basis before he became a regular member of the cast. Emerick, a Liverpudlian, played main character Mick Johnson in Brookside for many years and has had smaller roles in several other well-known television series. His Summer Wine character, PC Walsh was perhaps marginally the more gormless of the two timid law enforcement officers.

MALCOLM: 'The first policeman who was a major character was played by Matthew Kelly. He did a full week's filming with us around Marsden. A smashing fella. I knew Capstick well from Radio Sheffield; Kitson I got to know later on. They started off as minor characters and they'd be hanging around for hours waiting to do their bits. Then they started coming into the storylines

Sitting on a stone-built bit of a wall
(Malcolm Howarth)]

more and more. In a roundabout way, those two were involved in a news story that got into the local paper. There was an episode in the early 1990s involving a giant stuffed panda. It was a present for Howard from Marina. The two coppers were driving up on the moors talking about panda cars and one of them says, "It's not often you see a panda up here." At that moment they look out of the window and the show's three main men are sitting on a stone-built bit of wall with a huge black and white teddy bear. Then, as Ken Kitson approached the wall on foot, he sank up to his waist in a ditch, and as he did so he looked around and the men had disappeared.

'To achieve this, the BBC special effects department dug a trench by the wall, filled it with clean water, added cork to make it look muddy, placed a board on

top drilled full of holes, and disguised it with a grass sod, so when Kitson stood on it the water would come up through the holes and the ground would appear to be sinking underneath his feet. It worked very well but a few days before we filmed it, unknown to the BBC, a Holmfirth councillor had received a phone call from a constituent saying, "There's an old tanker up here on the moors and a suspicious-looking gang of men have just turned up in a van. I'm watching them now. They're dumping toxic waste on the moors!" An hour later, scientists in white forensic suits on were up on the tops, blocking the road and taking samples. A reporter from the Holme Valley Express got hold of this information and became very excited. It was the biggest story he'd ever done, and he persuaded the editor to run it on the front page. I got

Peter Sallis, Malcolm Howarth, Bill Owen, George Chakiris, and Brian Wilde in Extra! Extra!, 1996
(Malcolm Howarth)

wind of this and rushed into the office on the Thursday afternoon, just as they were going to press. I said, "Hold it, it's a Summer Wine stunt." But nobody wanted to know. The reporter held his hand up to my face to make me shut up. I didn't understand. There had been a criminal act. This was investigative journalism at work. I tried to explain that the so-called witness, the guy who had raised the alarm, had simply watched a hired tanker pumping clean water into a freshly dug ditch. The criminals in the van? The BBC special effects team. But by the time I got through to them it was too late – the presses had rolled. The reporter made a fool of himself, and the poor councillor as well. The editor was fuming.'

Lovelorn librarian and lifelong spinster Miss Lucinda Davenport was played by Josephine Tewson, a British comedy actress recognisable from roles in countless major television sitcoms and high-profile sketch shows from the 1960s onwards. Miss Davenport, who made her debut in a one-off appearance in 1997 and joined the cast proper in 2003, found kinship through a seemingly unlikely friendship with Marina. She would eventually fall in love with Luther 'Hobbo' Hobdyke, played by Russ Abbot.

MALCOLM: 'Josephine Tewson and Russ

Abbot were perfectly pleasant. Like a lot of well-known people, they came on board, did their bit, and didn't make a fuss about it. They blended in. George Chakiris is another good example. A big name in America, he was famous for being Bernardo in the movie West Side Story. He was in an episode called Extra! Extra! which featured a big circus set up. He had his own giant Winnebago and I thought here we go, big shot. But he was nothing of the sort. A completely normal guy, not full of himself in the slightest. Anything that was asked of him, including by me, he'd just get on and do it. He was great.'

While Jane Freeman continued playing Ivy, Kathy Staff left the show temporarily in May 2000, feeling the women in the cast were still not sufficiently valued in terms of their treatment on set. When she returned in 2003, she was given top billing on the opening credits, together with Frank Thornton and Peter Sallis.

MALCOLM: 'Kathy was respectful to everybody regardless of their position, and she didn't ever feel the need to put people down or in their place. No matter how junior someone was, she'd speak to them properly, like a human being. She was a devout Christian and that showed in her attitude. She was just one of those really nice people in life. Jane Freeman

was also a very pleasant woman, and not at all like her character. I had known her screen husband John Comer a little bit from way back, because he was a club turn as well as an actor, and I'd photographed him when I was working for the Wakefield City Sun.'

From series 25 onwards in 2004, Norman Clegg's roles were gradually reduced. By this time Peter Sallis was very much the father of the series, caring about it deeply. And although Sallis did not love Holmfirth like Bill Owen, he appreciated it, and found the Holme Valley countryside mesmerisingly beautiful. He also appreciated the quality of Roy Clarke's writing and having a tremendous supporting cast around him. Last Of The Summer Wine had, in many ways, become much more than just a job to him.

ON BORROWED TIME

Since the 1990s there had been rumblings emanating from the corridors of power at the BBC that Last Of The Summer Wine had run its course. Yet remarkably, periods of adversity and forced changes over the years had invariably helped rejuvenate the show rather than kill it. Its weekly audience now sat at under six million, but with many more television channels available and increasing internet access, this was still more

"Oooh Howard!"
"Oooh Marina!"

(Malcolm Howarth)

Shocking! Whatever it is, it's all about the eyelines
(Malcolm Howarth)

Miserly Marsden Junk shop proprietor, Auntie Wainwright
(Malcolm Howarth)

than many new sitcoms. Summer Wine was a great survivor, the last in a line of family comedy half-hours that once formed the solid bedrock of British light entertainment. But the show had not only survived the passing of most of British comedy's old guard; it had also outlived numerous new sitcoms, some of them already classics themselves, such as Only Fools And Horses and Blackadder, as well as the careers of many so-called alternative comedians.

But times were changing again, and there was a sense of indifference about Summer Wine at the BBC, and a renewed perception that, in some quarters within the corporation, people actively wanted to kill off the show. Some younger executives were snooty about the programme, looking down their noses at it, and every year its actors were dying or becoming too old to continue performing. It is fair to say that Last Of The Summer Wine had become a comedy backwater. More than ever its viewers were older people, many of them senior citizens. But children loved the antics of the show's elderly protagonists, with fan mail from kids frequently arriving at Television Centre, much of it addressed to Howard and Marina. Grandparents were watching with their grandchildren. What was wrong with that?

It was family entertainment. The humour was good natured, non-offensive and free of swearing. It was laugh out loud. It was non-aggressive, innocent, escapist, and silly. But it was still clever and wry and human. Importantly, the audience laughed with the characters rather than at them. The dialogue was as off the wall as ever, and important issues were discussed, albeit with a light touch. Comedy, of course, can be a highly effective and intelligent way of making a serious point.

Somehow the show kept finding its feet and moving forward. Budgets were reduced so stunts and crazy inventions were increasingly off limits, and with health and safety now becoming a limiting factor for a show with an elderly cast, there could be less outdoor action in general. So, in a further reinvention, Roy Clarke took the programme back to its beginnings, with dialogue carrying more of the story. Dora Bryan left the show after shooting the 2005 series. Keith Clifford left the next year of his own volition. Stephen Lewis left in 2007 due to illness. That year the audience had reduced further, to around 4.5 million. To add perspective, most current BBC comedies did no better, excepting The Vicar of Dibley, which attracted 12 million viewers.

By now Peter Sallis's eyesight was failing, and it was getting expensive to insure the older actors for outdoor shooting. Consequently, 2007 was the last year some of the cast were required on location, with their exterior scenes being created digitally. Frank Thornton was particularly peeved, and as Clegg once said, "The thing about growing old is you get fewer scabs on your knees but more internal injuries."

In October that year, the show's composer Ronnie Hazlehurst died aged 79. For future shows Alan Bell decided to re-use surviving recordings of Hazlehurst's incidental music, rather than commission another arranger to imitate his work.

A FINAL REINVENTION

Despite everything there was a mood of optimism among those who remained, even a feeling of renewal. But Kathy Staff would soon be gone too. She struggled to remember her lines during shooting in 2007 and was not well enough to film during 2008. She died from brain cancer at the end of that year. Her character, Nora Batty, was mourned across the nation, and Staff too, especially in her home town of Duckinfield.

Nora had become as much a part of Yorkshire as Betty's Tea Rooms or its heraldic white rose, and a modern variation of a historic British comedy staple, following a trail blazed by those such as Hattie Jacques, Dandy Nichols and Peggy Mount. In Summer Wine Land, Nora did not die; instead she went to Australia to stay with family. Brian Wilde also died in 2008, aged 80, following a fall at his home.

MALCOLM: 'I always got on very well with Brian Wilde. I did a small personal photo album for Brian when he was on the programme, and I was talking to him again about pictures just a few weeks before he died. The cast would often ask me for photographs. It's nice for them to have pictures at home or for their friends and family. And I did a lot of the portraits the BBC printed out as postcards with a space at the bottom for the actor's signature. I didn't charge for those, but some bigger jobs would leave me out of pocket. But it's strange, while all the really big names would always insist on paying for everything, the more minor ones would often take advantage. They thought they could get away with it because of their fame. I owed them the favour. They were actors in Last Of The Summer Wine you know! But the likes of Brian, Bill Owen and Peter Sallis would never let that happen. If I did anything for them that put me even slightly out of pocket, they'd offer to pay. Many times I'd refuse, but I couldn't always afford to say no.'

Following the departure of Billy Hardcastle in 2007, a new male main character was brought in. Introduced in the New Year's Eve special broadcast on December 31, 2008, entitled I Was A Hitman For Primrose Dairies was Luther

The indomitable Auntie Wainwright (Jean Alexander) with Smiler (Stephen Lewis) and Auntie Ros (Dora Bryan)
(Malcolm Howarth)

'Hobbo' Hobdyke, a former milkman and Clegg's new next-door neighbour. Hobbo was another nutcase in the Summer Wine tradition. Convinced he had once been a secret spy with MI5 links, a sort-of 008, he was always on the lookout for enemy attack and reminisced about leaping from aeroplanes on special assignments. Now his mission was to form a band of volunteers, on stand-by to react to emergencies, and Alvin and Entwistle were his first recruits.

Hobbo was played by comedian Russ Abbot, a massive television star in the 1980s headlining peak-time sketch shows that appealed to audiences of all ages. In many ways an old-school comic, Abbot could tell jokes, do impressions, sing, and play musical instruments, and use his tall, gangling frame to good advantage in physical comedy. He was also an excellent straight actor. Brought in when Sallis and Thornton were taken

off location shooting, Abbot was able to do stunts and take falls, and he brought a physical dimension to the programme not seen since Bill Owen's time. Like a young Foggy, Hobbo was a deluded man of action, fired by naive enthusiasm and pent-up energy.

For reasons that were never explained, Hobbo was convinced Pearl's friend Nelly was his mother. Nelly was played by yet another hugely recognisable British television star, Dame June Whitfield. One of the coffee morning group, which had endured despite changes of personnel down the years, Nelly was perhaps more worldly-wise than her female friends. Whitfield first appeared in Last Of The Summer Wine in 2008 along with Warren Mitchell, of Until Death Us Do Part fame, and then became a regular character. Mitchell played Potts, a hapless polar explorer, with Whitfield as his bossy wife. Once she became a regular, Nelly was frequently seen administering instructions and advice via mobile telephone to her apparently wholly inept and forever unseen husband, Travis. Whitfield had a long and successful career which ranged over time from Take It From Here on BBC Radio in 1953, via Hancock, all the way through to Absolutely Fabulous with Jennifer Saunders and Joanna Lumley, via The Goodies and Dick Emery. For a great number of years, she was comedian Terry Scott's on-screen wife in successful sitcoms including Terry and June.

Following Hobbo's debut episode which started Series 30, ten further new episodes were broadcast during 2009. With Clegg and Truly increasingly consigned to cameos, the show was headed by an all-male trio once again; this time comprising Hobbo, Alvin and Entwistle. Hobbo, the leader and an obviously comic figure, was given a lot of lines and plenty to do. Entwistle became more Clegg-like as the dry observer of absurdity all around, and chirpy Alvin was the man in the middle. Barry sometimes became involved in the main trio's schemes.

Nora Batty was replaced at 28 Huddersfield Road by her sister Stella, a redheaded former pub landlady played by Barbara Young, a Yorkshire actress who had previously appeared in the

Nora Batty
(Jenny Hinchliffe)

show with comedian Bobby Ball as an entirely different character, Florrie. Stella slotted into the coffee morning line-up while Glenda, no longer in her mother's shadow, was becoming more assertive. Ivy scolded the new leading trio as vituperatively as she had the originals, and Howard, Marina and Pearl's storylines were as barmy and doomed to failure as ever. The avaricious Auntie Wainwright also continued much as before.

Guest stars continued to appear, some staying to join the regular cast. Pompous golf club captain Toby Mulberry was played with aplomb by Trevor Bannister, previously best known for playing ladies' man Mr Lucas in Are You Being Served?, the 1970s sitcom. Mulberry's sidekick, Morton Beemish (first known as Herman Teesdale), was a nervy debt collector who hounded Tom Simmonite doggedly, but without success. Beemish was played by Christopher Beeny, who starred as a teenager in Britain's first ever television soap, The Grove Family, in the 1950s. He was known for having played footman Edward in popular early 1970s drama series Upstairs Downstairs, and Thora Hird's dim nephew in Yorkshire Television's period sitcom In Loving Memory. Cannon and Ball appeared in three shows. Radio veteran and music hall guru Roy Hudd played long-lost Lionel back in 2004. London comedian Brian Conley played Barry's annoying neighbour, fitness fanatic Boothroyd in 2008, and a year earlier comedy great Eric Sykes guest starred as Doggy, an elderly man getting remarried who has a stag do arranged for him. Sykes wrote for the great names of British comedy from the early 1960s onwards, including Tony Hancock, and Spike Milligan, and achieved recognition as a comedy actor for his work with Hattie Jacques.

Despite attracting these famous names, the show's future hung in the balance, even while series 30 was being broadcast to audiences of around three million during 2009. Finally, possibly reluctantly, a short series of six episodes was commissioned in May that year. Before this, word had got out that the show was being axed, prompting 800 letters of protest. That the BBC did not understand its own show was generally the gist. Roy Clarke set to work sensing correctly these would be the last scripts of an incredible run of programmes. And as the cast acted their parts during a short filming schedule of just four weeks in August and September 2009, they sensed it too. The interiors were recorded at Shepperton Studios in October, and at the preview screenings at Teddington Burt Kwouk, Jean Fergusson, Robert Fyfe and Russ Abbot appeared on stage to entertain the audience.

The demise of Last Of The Summer Wine was announced on June 2,

2010, before the final series of six was transmitted in July and August. Subsequently, special editions of Songs Of Praise and Countryfile were recorded in Holmfirth by way of tribute. To have written 295 episodes of a single television series over 37 years, and to a consistently excellent standard, was an incredible achievement by Roy Clarke. Some American shows have racked up more screen time, but these have always been written by writing teams and never by one person. And Last Of The Summer Wine outlived by far all the other great comedy shows from what was arguably British television's golden era; such wonderful series as Dad's Army, Fawlty Towers, Are You Being Served?, The Good Life, The Liver Birds, Steptoe and Son, and Porridge.

What, apart from Clarke's writing, were the secrets of its success? Small things make a difference. Costumes were generally consistent from show to show and series to series, with effort made to make them timeless. The show was pioneering in the extensive use of locations, and it was the first sitcom to spawn feature-length specials, which became an eagerly anticipated event at Christmas. Composer Ronnie Hazlehurst must also receive due credit. The programme's signature tune is sweet and tender, yet with an expansive, outdoor

Permanently on the lookout is Luther Hobbo Hobdyke (Russ Abbot)
(Malcolm Howarth)

Soldiering on: Truly (Frank Thornton) and Clegg (Peter Sallis)
(Malcolm Howarth)

feel. It is a beautiful piece of music and remains one of the most recognisable instrumental television themes ever. Was loyalty a factor? The show had many long-standing characters, and Jane Freeman and Peter Sallis stayed with the programme throughout its entire history. Furthermore, Alan Bell made the show his own, turning down office-bound promotions to stay at the helm.

Of course, the show lives on by way of DVD box sets, seemingly endless repeats on satellite and cable channels, and through streaming via Britbox. Summer Wine superfan Terry Bartlam's highly professional summerwine.net website attracts thousands of hits every month, and its forum has hundreds of active members from countries all over the world. All around the globe, fans chuckle along at their favourite characters, and beyond nostalgic rediscovery, the show's merits are constantly being ascertained and appreciated by new audiences, some surprisingly young in years. The programme's legacy is that new devotees can be made aware that wit, intelligence and humanity have a place in television comedy, and that for millions of older viewers over many years, the show's ageing characters and their stories have encouraged several generations to get out and about and experience fun and adventure, even as age takes its toll and their lives seemingly become more restricted.

What could possibly go wrong?
(Malcolm Howarth)

Alan Bell, the driving force behind the show for nearly 30 years
(Malcolm Howarth)

Chapter Nine

LEGACY FOR A NORTHERN TOWN

It is now more than ten years since the last episodes of Last Of The Summer Wine were filmed in and around Holmfirth, and nearly 50 since James Gilbert and his cast and crew turned up there to film the first ever story, Of Funerals And Fish, and sheltered from the rain in the Elephant and Castle pub. What has been the show's legacy for the tough little south Pennines market town?

Summer Wine-related tourism is less frantic than in the giddy days of the 1980s and early 1990s, but people still visit on day trips and for holidays, some making once-in-a-lifetime visits from abroad to do so.

Malcolm Howarth's Summer Wine exhibition is now sited in Compo's underdwelling on Scar Fold, immediately next door to the Summer Wine Shop which continues to sell his photographs among other souvenirs. Above the shop, the Wrinkled Stocking Tea Room now thrives under the auspices of Den and Jackie Fussell, and Nora's home, 28 Huddersfield Road, is a popular themed holiday let and shrine to the character and the series. Location bus tours depart from the parish church in the centre of Holmfirth and are run by Colin Frost, the former proprietor of Sid's Cafe. The cafe itself remains a key Summer Wine visitor destination and is now run by local lass Laura Booth.

And as well as being a magnet for dedicated fans of the programme, the area is well and truly on the map for walkers and cyclists keen to explore the spectacular countryside around the town. Holiday cottages and bed and breakfast establishments in and around Holmfirth provide a base for exploring the wider Summer Wine region; places such as the National Mining Museum, the Standedge Tunnel, and the town of Marsden. The nearby textile towns of Huddersfield and Halifax are both a short drive away, and the cities of Leeds and Bradford are within reach for a day visit. In these places further remnants of Yorkshire's industrial heritage can still be found and explored. In the evenings a number of pubs and bars and several good restaurants provide

Holmfirth plate by Jenny Hinchliffe
(Howard Allen)

Looking to the future
(Malcolm Howarth)

good quality sustenance and refreshment in Holmfirth. For traditionalists, Compo's Cafe and Hollowgate Fisheries provide classic fish and chips.

Holmfirth is also considerably smarter in appearance than in days of yore. Established in the 13th century, it has always been an unsentimental little town, a hardy settlement built on wool, mills, and dye works. By 1973 the textile industry was in retreat and Holmfirth was starting to look down at heel. But tourism became its new industry and an engine of renewal and as visitor numbers grew, the town smartened itself up. Now it is principally a commuter town, and a pleasant place in which people can work from home. Like all British towns, Holmfirth has

Big stars gone. St. John's Church, Upperthong, Holmfirth
(Howard Allen)

to deal with bank branch closures, the rising popularity of home shopping, and other changes which affect its centre. There are no working mills, few surviving dye works and less industry in general, and Holmfirth's residents and business owners must find ways forward following the coronavirus epidemic of 2020. But like Last Of The Summer Wine, reinvention has always been a Holmfirth trait.

JENNY HINCHLIFFE: 'Summer Wine changed the town's direction and gave it a new lease of life. People took more pride in their home town because people were coming in numbers to see it and making a fuss, saying how special it was. Some people pretended they didn't like it, but it has changed the town beyond belief. People painted their houses, the shops were done up, and new businesses opened, it was like the place had a facelift. Some people can be very snobby, but Summer Wine has given Holmfirth a sense of self-esteem which has been building up now for more than 40-odd years. Most people won't remember what it was like to walk down Hollowgate then. I can remember people coming out from bingo in the Picturedrome cinema, sitting on the bench eating fish and chips, and counting the rats across the river. The town was definitely on its uppers a bit before Last Of The Summer Wine, but I really liked it. I liked the people I came across who were a bit off the wall... a bit unusual, if you like, and even though it was a bit dingy, I soon fell in love with the place. I couldn't believe you could knock on somebody's door and

they'd shout, "Come in luv!" and they'd somehow know who it was! A place like Holmfirth changes all the time. That's why it's difficult to put your finger on the character of it, and it's changing again now with so many people coming in from London and other places. But as things change it retains some of its old character. Part of that, I think, is because it's in a valley. It's enclosed, and that leads to a feeling of community.'

JACK DUNNILL: 'Even now there are comments on the Holmfirth History website from a small minority of people saying Summer Wine ruined Holmfirth. But broadly speaking, Summer Wine has been of great benefit. It has brought about the gentrification of the town, very much so. It's made it a desirable place to live which has, in turn, attracted people who are keen to improve the place further still. The price of houses is strong as a result and always a bit ahead of other areas around Huddersfield.'

BERYL DUNNILL: 'The programme's legacy is that it has brought a great deal of pleasure to millions of people around the world, and that everywhere you go people have heard of Holmfirth. We've travelled extensively and as soon as people find out where we're from they invariably tell us how much they have enjoyed the programme. People from Canada, Australia, South Africa, you name it.'

MALCOLM: 'The show was originally going to be in the Open All Hours area

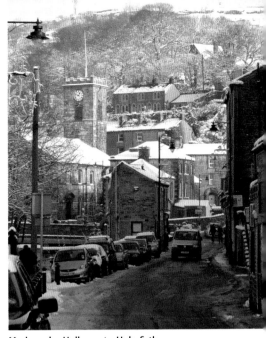
Modern-day Hollowgate, Holmfirth
(Jean Shires)

of Doncaster. If it had gone ahead there, I don't think Summer Wine would have lasted as long. Open All Hours was a better fit there and Holmfirth was perfect for Summer Wine Land. It's the scenery that's done it, and the character of Holmfirth. The town's been good for the show and the show's been good for the town.'

JENNY: 'It's a sort-of eccentric place. I really think it's one of the most individual and unusual small towns in the country, and it's forever evolving into something else. And when Last Of The Summer Wine is no longer being screened at all, it will become something else again.'

PHOTOGRAPHIC MEMORIES

Summer Wine photographer Malcolm Howarth is retired now after a long second career that came about due to a series of happy accidents. This is his story.

'I'm a Barnsley lad. I'm not from Holmfirth, but I started to go there regularly as a freelance photographer working for the Holme Valley Express, and that's how I got to know people from Last Of The Summer Wine. Before I became a photographer, I was a fully qualified mechanical engineer and worked in an engineering workshop for many years, but I couldn't stand being shut in. I needed fresh air, and when I had my appendix out and I was off work for six weeks, I lay there thinking about things and decided to make a break. I was offered an outdoor job for a friend of mine who sold pre-packed potatoes, which was a new thing at that time. I earned some good money but I had to be out in all weathers and I thought, I haven't done all this training to finish up being a potato salesman. I'd always been into photography and was already doing weddings for some of the top high street photographers

at the time, and it got to the point where I was doing three weddings every weekend. Again, the money was okay but working every weekend wasn't ideal. So, I thought, if I'm being paid for taking photographs I might as well start doing it for a living.

'I was still doing a lot of weddings to start with so I didn't get my weekends back straight away, but because I'd got all week spare, through a friend of mine I got into press photography, starting off by freelancing for the Wakefield City Sun and the Pontefract and Castleford Sun, and then the Holme Valley Express. They were proper local newspapers in those days, not like the regional press is now. Putting everything together, I was just about making a living. But this was a time when Page Three was beginning to become a thing in national newspapers. Glamour photography, they called it, and it was more innocent then – not how it ended up. The girl would perhaps have a fella's shirt on, and the shirt would be open down the middle, and that's as far as it went. I did one or two of those and it paid very well. I could earn a fortnight's money for one

Malcolm Howarth
(Wes Hobson)

picture. But it wasn't long before specialist London agencies took over.

'Meanwhile I did hundreds of jumble sales, am-dram first nights, shop openings, prize-givings... all sorts of local events. That was my bread and butter, and I was coming over to Holmfirth quite a bit. I already knew the place a

A special presentation to Bill Owen at Pinewood Studios commemorating his part in the first 25 years of Last Of The Summer Wine. Left to right: Malcolm Howarth, Peter Sallis, Bill Owen, Don Smith, and Brian Wilde
(Malcolm Howarth)

Last orders! Marina has designs on Smiler while landlord Ron Backhouse looks on
(Malcolm Howarth)

little because my uncle used to be the caretaker of Holmfirth Swimming Baths, an outdoor pool up Rotcher near the town centre. It's still there actually, although I wouldn't go diving in – there isn't any water in it! I got into professional photography at the right time. Large format cameras were going out and smaller cameras that took 35mm film were coming in. Before then if you wanted a good quality picture you needed a big camera which took 2.25" images. And some of the really old guys were still using cameras with glass plates slotted in the back. The negative size of a 35mm camera may have been much smaller than in these older types but the quality was there if you knew how to use them, and I found I could do a lot of in-camera special effects older photographers didn't want to bother with.

'Then, later on in the 1970s, really good long lenses started coming in. That made a big difference on some jobs. For years I'd cover football matches at Huddersfield Town and Barnsley FC, sometimes both on the same afternoon, moving between the two grounds at half-time. For years I spent my Saturday afternoons getting freezing cold and soaking wet through, squatting uncomfortably on my camera case by the side of a goal. It was dangerous too. We were told, "Don't move. They'll run past or jump over you." They didn't always. I regularly got walloped by the ball and clattered by big men running full pelt.

'One Christmas fixture at Barnsley, a player smacked the ball into my face from near point-blank range. Luckily, I'd just lowered the camera. There was a crunch and I thought, "I'm dying". The next thing I knew I was lying on my back seeing stars, with the Barnsley captain leaning over, asking if I was alright. I'd been out cold for four minutes and the referee had stopped the game. Then at the end of the match there was controversy because the ref only allowed one minute of injury time. But the pain and discomfort was all worth it when my team, Barnsley, were promoted to the Premier League for the 1997/8 season.

'For many years I used an Olympus, which was a very neat, well-engineered, professional camera that you could take to bits in a minute: lens in one pocket, camera body in another, and nobody would know you were carrying it.

Handy for court rooms and other situations. Contax were the bees' knees and I had one of those too, but they never really caught on with the Press in a big way, probably because the motordrives on the Canons were superior. Canons took over for a long period then Nikons dominated the market. Of course, the technology eventually changed again. Film went out and I went over to digital for the last few years of my press work. I had to because I was freelancing a lot for the Huddersfield Examiner. They were always streamlining, and new technology was a part of that. I had to be compatible with the Examiner so when I turned 60, I had to buy new equipment and start learning again. The worst bit was inputting caption details in the camera rather than writing them out by hand. I'd be doing seven or eight jobs on a night, then having to type out with one finger the names of football teams, am-dram casts and goodness knows what else, so I'd be late home or to the pub which wasn't fair!

'Anyone who wants to be a professional photographer these days is up against it because everybody and their grandmother has a camera now. You hardly ever see proper wedding photographers, and reporters take their own pictures. The equipment's made the job easier but in some ways, it's become harder to make a living. You must have a good artistic eye, which is not my particular strength, actually. I'm not so good at still life. Not my forte. But I can set a scene up to tell a story. I can set a press picture up, and more often than not it will work out reasonably well. Don't get me wrong, I've done some rubbish in my time, but I am capable of doing a good job. It's about having an eye for the situation. With digital cameras you can see what you're getting straight away, but in the days of film you couldn't see your results. I used to bracket the exposures just to be sure, but I used to have competitions with myself. I'd look out of the window and say right, on 400 asa film that's a 250th at f16 and I'd be right. I got so that I didn't need a light meter but there are situations you can't go back to.

'I photographed Cliff Richard for the BBC's Holiday programme at locations all around the Harrogate area. I was with him all day and

everything depended on me getting it right. Cliff is a really super bloke. Great to work with and as nice as you could wish. But I was nervous, I don't mind admitting it. At that time, you could never depend on automatic exposures. I'd take a couple of automatic shots and then I'd set the camera up to what I thought would be the best settings. I had to know exactly what I was doing because I couldn't afford to get it wrong. Then if necessary, I'd go in with a light meter but not making it obvious, I'd be chatting with them and just checking it casually. I never made it an issue.

'Around the same time, I spent a week at Birmingham airport filming an episode of the Holiday programme with another lovely person, Jill Dando. She was learning to be an air hostess and she qualified within a week, getting her golden wings quicker than anyone else had ever done it. Of course, her training was arranged so she could achieve that, but she actually passed her exam. That afternoon she said to me, "Right Malcolm, we're off to Florida." So I went with her on a flight to Florida on a 747 while she did her first shift as an air hostess, taking stills of her in action and documenting the story. The only problem was I never got out of the flaming airport! Other jobs I did for the BBC as a result of doing Summer Wine included several days on The Fast Show with Paul Whitehouse, Charlie Higson and Mark Williams. Smashing guys, all of them.

'I've never been pushy. I've always tried to be involved with stuff that's been of interest and for me my work has not just been about making a living. If I hadn't enjoyed being a photographer, I wouldn't have done it in the first place, or stuck with it for so many years. I had a heart attack when I was 65, just after the Examiner went through yet another round of cuts and I was moved out with the furniture. When I recovered, I decided it was time to call it a day. I enjoyed the human side of the job. First and foremost, being the Last Of The Summer Wine photographer was all about working with people. I'm retired now and I do voluntary work with young people. I enjoy doing that because there's a purpose behind it. It's not just a duty or a job. I'm not getting paid for it, although I sometimes think that's what I've done wrong in life, I've never thought enough about money!'